# TOXIC COPS

D1518925

# D. J. ARNESON

# TOXIC COPS

FRANKLIN WATTS
NEW YORK/LONDON/TORONTO/SYDNEY
A VENTURE BOOK/1991

Photographs courtesy of: Photo Researchers: pp. 11 (Laurence Pringle), 17 (Verna R. Johnston), 23 (Nancy J. Pierce), 27 (Alexander Lowry), 32 (J. Pavlovsky/Rapho), 39 (Robert Perron), 66 (Patrick Grace), 69 (Ray Ellis), 75 (Eugene Gordon); NASA: p. 14; U.S. Geological Survey: p. 20; Animals Animals/ Earth Scenes: pp. 31 (Wendy Neefus), 35 (Tony Allen/OSF); Gamma-Liaison: pp. 50 (Leloup/Figaro), 86 (John Chiasson); Exxon Company: p. 57; U.S. Environmental Protection Agency: pp. 58, 104 (Steve Delaney); New York Department of Sanitation, Environmental Police Unit: pp. 81, 96.

Library of Congress Cataloging-in-Publication Data

Arneson, D. J.
Toxic cops / D.J. Arneson.
p. cm. — (A Venture book)
Includes bibliographical references and index.
Summary: Discusses several threats to the environment, laws that have been enacted to protect it, and the branch of the Environmental Protection Agency and other local groups that enforce such laws.
ISBN 0-531-12525-4
1. Offenses against the environment—United States—Juvenile literature. [1. Offenses against the environment. 2. Pollution.]
I. Title.
HV6403.A76 1991
363.7—dc20                                           90-13102 CIP AC

# CONTENTS

# TOXIC COPS

# INTRODUCTION

This is the story of what is happening to our planet. Your planet. It begins in outer space and ends in your backyard.

But the story doesn't really stop there because it has no ending. Not yet. It's like the tales of *The Arabian Nights,* in which the storyteller weaves a new story every day, to save her life. In other words, new chapters that keep its people's fate uncertain are being added to earth's story.

How the story will end is going to depend on how much the people of the world—5 billion and growing by tens of thousands every day—want to preserve their planet and are willing to do something about it. Some are already working harder than most to make sure that earth's story never ends. They are America's Environmental Enforcement police, the nation's "Toxic Cops."

Toxic Cops are a small, select group of men and women in a few federal and municipal departments scattered across the United States who are dedicated to preserving the planet. Not many people have ever heard of them or the work they do. Much of what they do is ordinary. Like police officers, fire fighters, and FBI and drug enforcement agents, Toxic Cops don't make headlines every day. And like detectives on a case, they may spend months of slow, careful investigation to bring their quarry to justice, only to lose in court on a legal formality. That doesn't happen often, but it does happen. When it does, they go right back to work, harder than ever, to make sure that the next time an offender is charged with a crime the charge will stick.

Toxic Cops investigate a new breed of criminal lawbreakers: planetary polluters. Planetary polluters are not astronauts who toss garbage out of orbiting satellites to litter the sky with space junk— they would be easy to catch. The real planetary polluters live right down here with the rest of us.

Planetary polluters are the people and companies that fill the sky with the sulfuric smoke that makes acid rain. They pour into rivers and lakes chemical wastes that kill fish and toxify the water.

*Since the beginning of the Industrial Revolution, enormous amounts of pollution have been released into the atmosphere. These smokestacks along the New Jersey Turnpike are a graphic illustration of this.*

They dump polluting garbage into the sea. They bury in the earth hazardous substances that poison wells and people. They dispose of infected needles and medical waste that foul beaches. They are the people who knowingly or unknowingly treat the environment as their personal garbage can.

Of course, Toxic Cops can't protect the whole planet. Earth is much too big and the danger of its destruction much too widespread. And the story really doesn't begin on earth, but in outer space.

# 1
# THE ECOSPHERE

When earth is viewed from space, its limits are as sharply defined as a lonely wooden raft on an endless empty sea. It is all there is. And like castaways on a raft, the people of earth have no place to go to get more of what they need in order to survive. Luckily, everything that we need is already on the planet.

Earth is "the water planet," called that because three-fourths of its surface is covered with water. No other planet in our solar system has it. Without water, earth would be as dead and lifeless as all the other planets.

Earth could also be called the "air planet" because it has a unique atmosphere. Other planets have atmospheres, but earth's air—a combination of nitrogen, oxygen, and traces of other gases—supports life.

*This fantastic view of earth as photographed from the Apollo 17 spacecraft shows the Mediterranean Sea area to the Antarctic south polar ice cap.*

These two one-of-a-kind oceans surround the earth. The ocean of water hugs the planet so closely that only scattered islands of land—real islands and giant continents—poke through. The ocean of air lies like a blanket over everything, towering so high that not even the tallest mountains can pierce it. Above the blanket of air is endless space. Together, water and air form a shallow layer around the earth called the *ecosphere.*

Within the ecosphere, between the thin air at the edge of space and the sunless depths of the ocean bottom, is all the life on earth there is. It is probably all the life in our entire solar system, and possibly all the life in the whole universe.

## Life-Forms in the Ecosphere

Charles Darwin was one of the first scientists to study the diversity and variety of living things. When he traveled the globe on the ship, the *Beagle,* gathering specimens and data, he was amazed at the variety of life he found. But he had no idea of the true numbers of things that live together within the narrow bounds of earth's wispy ecosphere.

The voyage of the *Beagle* lasted from 1831 to 1836. Today, over a century and a half later—an eye-blink in the history of the planet—scientists estimate that there are from *5 to 30 million* different life-forms on earth. The animals are not all as magnificent as lions or as intelligent as apes, as large as elephants or as graceful as birds. The insects are not all as busy as ants or as hardy as cockroaches, as creative as spiders or as tiny as

15

mites. The plants are not all as tall as redwoods or as colorful as flowers, as simple as lichen or as ordinary as weeds. In fact, most living things aren't even known. Only about 1.7 million have been catalogued. The rest remain a mystery.

Almost everything—more than 90 percent—that has ever lived on earth has become extinct. To be extinct does not mean that something, a monkey, for example, dies. It means that that *kind* of monkey—all of them—has died everywhere and that there will never be another one like it again. The more than 30 million life-forms living today represent only what has survived through evolution. How many different forms have actually lived since life began 4 billion years ago will never be known.

Ordinarily, from prehistoric times on, living things become extinct at a rate of about one species every ten days. Today it is estimated that as many as 100 species will become extinct *every day.*

What on earth is happening?

## Climate and Weather

The earth's average temperature is about 60° Fahrenheit (15.5° Celsius). That's roughly what the outside air feels like on a cool summer evening in most places in the United States. If you were going outside, you might wear a light jacket or sweater to be comfortable.

Of course, averages include the most and the least of something. The average temperature at the North and South poles is not 60° Fahrenheit, and 60° Fahrenheit is not the average temperature at the equator. Each place has its own average tem-

There would seem to be nothing in common between
the giant Sierran redwood and a small plant
like a fern, but they all go through the
process of photosynthesis to manufacture food.
The Sierran redwood (Sequoia gigantea) *may
live for more than 3,000 years.*

perature. The average temperature and weather for a particular place is called its *climate*.

There is always a big difference between the climates at the top and bottom of the globe and the climate around its middle. This is due to the angle of the sun's rays as they strike the earth. The rays that hit the earth's midsection are like a punch in the stomach. The rays that reach the poles are like a glancing blow to the head. Much more energy—heat—collects in the middle compared to the small amount that collects on each end.

The sun is the source of virtually all of the heat on earth, either as direct sunlight or as stored energy in plant matter and fossil fuels. Fossil fuels can affect the weather, but ordinary everyday weather, the kind you see outside right now, is produced by the heat of the sun. Very little heat from the sun reaches the earth's poles. Huge amounts of the sun's heat reach the equator.

Climate differences—sharp contrasts between cold air and hot air—make weather. Hot air rises because it expands, or gets lighter (think of smoke billowing out of a smokestack). Cold air sinks because it contracts, or gets heavier (think of how your bare feet feel the cold when you open the refrigerator door). Moving air is wind.

The cold air capping the poles clings to the earth because it is heavy. The warm air around the middle of the earth rises because it is light. When the caps of polar air grow colder and deeper, they become too heavy to support themselves. The cold air begins to flow over the globe like a pile of whipped cream on top of an apple. It pushes away the warm air that is already rising. The result is that the thick ocean of air surrounding the earth—its atmosphere—is constantly moving. The general movement of air flows from west to east because the earth is spinning on its axis like a giant top in space. Locally, however, the wind and weather can blow in any direction.

When warm air passes over water, or land that is moist, water vapor joins the mass of air rising into the sky. As the air rises, it cools and begins to contract. The water vapor inside is squeezed into a smaller and smaller space until it condenses to form tiny droplets of water. The droplets bump into one another and grow into larger drops. When a drop is too heavy to be supported by the air, it falls as rain or, if the air is cold enough, as hail or sleet or snow.

The earth's climate and weather patterns remain fairly constant over time. Many thousands of years pass between major climate changes. The planet was much warmer in prehistoric times, when volcanoes and other geologic factors were very active. It was much colder during the numerous ice ages that have occurred throughout its history. At the present time, earth's climate and weather are stable. However, there are disturbing signs that something unusual is causing unnatural changes. This upsets the old saying that you can talk about the weather but you can't do anything to change it. We may be changing the weather in ways that are out of control.

## The Greenhouse Effect

Outer space is bitterly cold. The warmth we feel on earth stays on earth because earth's atmosphere is like a giant, transparent blanket. The sun's

*Volcanic activity, such as this eruption
of Mt. St. Helens in Washington in 1980,
influences weather. Volcanic activity was at its
greatest during the mountain-building periods
that preceded the different ice ages.*

rays are able to shine through the blanket to strike the earth and everything on it. This is the heat we feel when lying on the beach or walking in direct sunlight.

However, when a cloud passes in front of the sun, we instantly feel cooler. If the air itself weren't warm, we would feel very cold indeed. But air holds heat. The problem is that air alone doesn't hold enough heat to support life on earth. If the blanket of air around the earth were all that kept us warm, we would soon freeze.

Luckily, earth's atmosphere contains carbon dioxide ($CO_2$). Sunlight, loaded with energy in the form of visible light, is able to pass through the carbon dioxide and reach the earth. Some of the energy is converted into heat that stays in the lower atmosphere, but most is reflected skyward as invisible infrared light. Carbon dioxide absorbs infrared energy, trapping it as heat inside the atmosphere in the same way heat from the sun is trapped inside a greenhouse.

If the carbon dioxide weren't there, the heat would dissipate into space and the temperature of the earth's surface would be about 0° Fahrenheit (−17.8° Celsius). Everything except hot springs and active volcanoes would be frozen. If there were a lot more carbon dioxide in the atmosphere, scarcely any heat would escape into space. Earth's climate would be quite a bit warmer from pole to pole. Just how warm would depend on the amount of carbon dioxide in the air.

For most of earth's history, changes in the amount of atmospheric carbon dioxide have occurred very slowly. Average surface temperatures have gone from hot to cold many times, but the period of time between one extreme and the other is measured in thousands of years. The life on earth has had plenty of time to adapt to the gradual changes. Some things failed to adapt, of course, and became extinct, but natural extinction rates rarely varied.

But a very short time ago in earth time, things began to change rapidly. Beginning with the dawn of the Industrial Revolution, about 200 years ago, enormous quantities of wood, coal, and natural gas have been burned to fuel factories that manufacture the goods people buy. To make anything from an axhead to a zoom lens takes energy. Whether the energy is used to feed a furnace to turn iron ore into steel, to generate electricity to power a milling machine, or to heat an oven to bake 10,000 loaves of bread, it has to come from somewhere.

Most of the energy used on earth comes from one of humankind's earliest discoveries—fire. Fire is an extremely active chemical reaction in which some kind of fuel rapidly combines with oxygen to produce heat and a number of by-products. A major by-product of burning earth's most abundant and cheapest fuels—wood, coal, oil, or natural

*Molten steel is poured from a huge furnace into a suspended tub, and will eventually emerge as steel bars. The fuel needed for this process will add carbon dioxide to the earth's atmosphere.*

gas—is carbon dioxide, the same carbon dioxide found naturally in the atmosphere. The more fuel burned, the more carbon dioxide produced.

From the beginning of the Industrial Revolution, burning fuel has released enormous amounts of carbon dioxide into the atmosphere. But not all of it stays there. If it did, the normal accumulation of carbon dioxide that has come from natural phenomena such as decomposing organic matter, volcanic activity, wildfires, and other events over billions of years would still be present. The atmosphere would be so full of carbon dioxide that most of the sun's energy would be trapped, and earth would be a hothouse. For example, Venus, our neighbor in space, has a thick cover of carbon dioxide which, along with other components in its atmosphere, keeps it baking at 850° Fahrenheit (454° Celsius).

But earth's carbon dioxide is recycled constantly. Much of the recycling is through plant photosynthesis. In photosynthesis, green plants take in carbon dioxide from the air and water from the soil, and in the presence of chlorophyll and sunlight produce glucose and give off oxygen. Trees are the most abundant source of photosynthesizers. Since forests and jungles are the places thickest with trees, they function to decrease the earth's carbon dioxide levels.

Two unnatural conditions have offset nature's recycling efforts. One is that people are consuming such huge amounts of energy that the volume of carbon dioxide that enters the atmosphere is increasing. The second is the fact that earth's forests are being cut down for fuel and building, for making paper pulp, or simply to clear the land for

24

grazing. Fewer trees means less carbon dioxide is being absorbed. So at a time when levels of carbon dioxide are increasing, the natural way for it to be absorbed—through photosynthesis—is decreasing.

Together, they mean that there is much more carbon dioxide in the air now than there was just 200 years ago. And the amount is building steadily and rapidly.

## Global Warming

Science is uncertain if the increased greenhouse effect of the past two centuries is actually heating the planet and, if so, if the rise in temperature is dangerous. Early predictions that global warming would melt ice caps, raise ocean levels, flood coastal cities, turn fertile lands into deserts, and make inhospitably cold regions comfortable places to live may be inaccurate.

Global warming may be only a natural temperature increase associated with little understood planetary "seasons." Some scientists think that small changes in the earth's orbit cause its temperature to rise and fall, although it takes thousands of years to do this. At one extreme would be an ice age or "winter," and at the other, a period of warming, or "summer." Right now, earth may be in a natural warming trend which, like ordinary spring, signals the coming of summer. To believe that civilization has permanently heated the entire atmosphere with its factories and automobiles may be as mistaken as to think that a bonfire on a cool spring evening causes summer.

## Ozone Depletion

In the upper regions of the protective atmospheric blanket surrounding the earth is a layer of ozone ($O_3$). Like carbon dioxide, ozone molecules act as a shield. The difference is that carbon dioxide traps *infrared* energy in and ozone keeps *ultraviolet* energy out. Ultraviolet light is the part of sunlight that causes fair-skinned people to sunburn. It is also believed to be the main cause of some kinds of skin cancer, and may be associated with eye cataracts and other physical disorders. Its dangers come from long exposure to it.

Ozone does such a good job of filtering sunlight that most ultraviolet light never reaches the earth. However, ozone is destroyed when it combines with chlorine, a chemical used in the manufacture of chlorofluorocarbons. Chlorofluorocarbons (CFCs) are good insulators and are used in many products, including Styrofoam and refrigeration coolants. For many years compressed CFC gases were used as propellants in spray cans of everything from hair spray to paint. Chlorofluorocarbons are still used to make the foam burger baskets common at many fast-food restaurants.

Chlorofluorocarbons can outlive people. Once they are released into the atmosphere, they can

*The aerosol waste cans here, in a hazardous waste-storage barrel in California, are one of the main culprits in the release of chlorofluorocarbons into the atmosphere.*

last 100 years or more. If you sprayed from a CFC-propelled can today, some of the molecules could still be around when your great-grandchildren are grown up. Fortunately, the dangers of CFCs in the atmosphere began to be recognized in the 1970s. Their use in spray cans was banned in the United States, even though many other countries still allow them. But even that may have been too late.

In 1985, scientists discovered a hole in the ozone layer over the South Pole. It is generally accepted that the hole was caused by CFCs in the upper atmosphere. The hole shrinks or grows depending on the weather, but it is as real as a bald spot on a man's head that would still be covered with hair if the unsuspecting victim had not sprayed it off himself.

Chlorofluorocarbon danger does not stop with its effects on the ozone layer. Chlorofluorocarbons also trap heat. In fact, a spray can of CFC molecules released into the atmosphere would hold 20,000 times more heat than the same number of molecules from a can of carbon dioxide. If the greenhouse effect is a real danger, CFCs add to it in a very big way.

# 2
# THE ECOSYSTEM

The surface of the earth is a wonderfully varied place. It is covered by seas and deserts, mountains and ice caps, and tundras and plains in an endless combination of geographical and climatic differences. Such rich diversity permits a mixture of environments that are able to support life forms numbering in the millions (5 to 30 million, as we said, though nobody knows for sure).

An environment is all of the conditions that affect the existence and growth of an organism or group of organisms. A fish tank, for example, is the environment for the fish living in it, a swamp is an environment for a frog, and a city is the environment for the people living there. An environment can have all, some, or none of the conditions necessary to sustain life. The conditions can be natural or human-made.

An ecosystem is an environment plus the community of plants, animals, and other organisms living together in it. In an ecosystem the environment and the things living in it are interrelated. A frog in a swamp catching a mosquito while sitting on a lily pad floating on the water is part of an ecosystem. The frog, the swamp, the mosquito, and the lily pad are all related to one another.

Each living thing in an ecosystem depends on everything else in it, even though the dependence may not be close or even obvious. When something causes a dramatic change in an ecosystem, some, part, or all of the system may die. Spilling oil on the swamp would kill the mosquito larvae living in the water. If the frog ate only mosquitos, it would either die or move to another swamp to obtain its food. The lily pad would probably survive, and perhaps the fish as well. Eventually the oil would vanish and the frog could return. However, if the balance of life in the swamp were delicate, the oil might kill the fish and the lily and change the environment so much that nothing could live in it again.

Ecosystems can be as tiny as a drop of water or as large as a jungle, and as different as rivers and deserts. When all of earth's ecosystems are taken together, they are like nested Chinese boxes, each one a part of a bigger system, going from the smallest to the largest. Each may seem to be independent, but when you remove any one of them, you remove a part of the whole.

## Oceans, Lakes, and Waterways

Water—salt water and fresh water—covers 70 percent of the planet. All life on earth began in the

*This great blue heron, in a woody swamp in New York, is only one part of the complex community of its ecosystem.*

primordial ocean formed when the planet cooled some 4 billion years ago. Water was the source of life in earth's beginning and remains the source of life today.

Ocean water is salty because of the accumulation of minerals over billions of years. Millions of life forms have adapted to seawater, from microscopic plankton at the bottom of the ocean food chain to mammoth whales near the top. The numbers, colors, sizes, and forms of aquatic life are so varied that they defy description. From simple one-celled plants and animals to creatures so bizarre they seem to be from another planet, the oceans of the earth teem with life.

Fresh water is not so abundant. Much of it is locked in polar ice caps. Large amounts of fresh water lie underground in unseen waterways and deep reservoirs called *aquifers.* Some very deep aquifers hold water thousands of years old. Others are replenished by water that falls to the ground as rain and soaks far into the earth.

The most familiar fresh water, except for that which comes from a faucet, is on the surface of the earth in ponds, lakes, streams, and rivers. The deepest freshwater lake, Lake Baikal in Russia, holds 20 percent of all the earth's fresh water. The Great Lakes in the United States also contain enormous amounts. A favorite fishing hole, neighborhood

*An oil spill, such as this one in France, can easily change the delicate balance of life in this particular ecosystem.*

33

pond, or the swamp with the frog hold scarcely any at all by comparison. But millions of ponds, swamps, and small lakes together add up to an ocean of fresh water. Connecting them is a network of creeks, streams, and rivers as widespread and intricate as all of the leaf veins on a giant tree. Just as the tiny veins in the smallest leaf on top of the tree are connected to the roots at the tree's bottom, so is all of earth's fresh water joined to the sea.

Water is in constant motion; even water in a placid lake does not stand still. Evaporation from the water's surface causes water molecules to rise into the air. Heat from the sun produces rising currents of air which carry the water vapor skyward. Eventually the water condenses and falls as rain or snow, and the endless cycle of evaporation and condensation continues.

Swamps and wetlands may hold the water for a while, and some water may soak deep into the ground. But eventually most water runs off the land into the network of creeks and streams that drain the land, pouring their water into larger lakes and rivers. Rivers join rivers and run downhill toward the sea.

## Landmasses

Once life-forms emerged from the sea, they conquered the land. Now there is scarcely a place on earth that does not harbor some form of life. Some life forms—humans are the best example—can live almost anywhere. Others have habitats that are so specialized they would perish if the smallest change

Fresh water is not as abundant as ocean water, and is found locked in polar ice caps and deep underground. The most familiar fresh water is found in lakes, the largest of which is Lake Baikal in southern Siberia.

were made. Over billions of years, life forms have adapted to the planet, but each adaptation is usually very specialized.

If every place in the entire world were exactly the same, down to the smallest chemical detail, it's possible that only one kind of life would ever have developed on earth. Variations through changes in hereditary material (mutation) or recombinations of hereditary material (sexual reproduction), would not have been necessary to ensure survival, and new species would not have evolved. Of course, the earth is anything but homogeneous. It is a collection of continents and islands with different ecosystems that spread around the globe, from pole to pole.

About 225,000,000 years ago, there was only one immense continent. Called Pangaea, it broke up the way an ice floe does in spring. Large chunks floating on a molten sea slowly drifted apart, propelled by rising currents of lava from the superhot core of the earth. Some pieces remained connected; others were separated by oceans. It is possible to walk from Alaska at the top of the North American continent to Tierra Del Fuego at the tip of South America, which is also a continent. Someone living at the southern tip of Africa could also walk to Siberia at the upper eastern edge of Asia, or to Lapland at the northernmost western edge of Europe. But Columbus had to sail a ship across the oceans to discover the Americas. And even today, it takes many hours at jet speeds to reach Australia from any other continent.

Separated by distance, whether they were once

connected or not, and by great differences in climate and topography, the earth's landmasses produced an incredible variety of environments. Some are inhospitable to most life forms. Others are home to an endless, and still uncataloged, assortment of living things. Plankton and penguins live in Antarctica, lions and giraffes dwell in the African plains, prehistoric coelacanths swim somewhere in the depths off the southern coast of Africa and Madagascar, jackrabbits bound across the grasslands of North Dakota, and possibly Nessie, the Loch Ness "monster," really does live at the bottom of that lake. Other life-forms—plants, bacteria, fungi—are just as diverse and far-flung—think of the mold growing in an old sneaker and a giant sequoia growing in California.

No environment is more important than the one in which you live. For a parrot, the polar ice is too remote to think about. A walrus would feel the same way about the jungle or a desert. People, however, can claim the whole world as their environment, and no place, no matter how far away or unlikely to be home, should be thought of as unimportant.

## Forests

The most majestic of plants are the trees. When they grow together in thick abundance that stretches beyond the horizon, they invite exploration to discover what lies beyond. But their size and density also creates a barrier that says nothing can pass. People have always lived at the edges of forests and rarely in them. When more room was needed, trees were cut down to make open space. The more space, the less forest.

For most of history, forests have been regarded as endless. Now, however, we know that all forests have two edges—one where they start and the other where they end. As the distance between the edges gets smaller, so do the forests. As forests decrease in size, their benefits to people and the planet diminish. It may be possible that everyone can survive on a planet without trees, but it is not the kind of experiment that should be undertaken or accident that should be allowed to happen.

Until recently, tropical rain forests were uncharted, unexplored places. Added together they cover about 7 percent of the globe, which isn't a lot compared with what's left. But within them live more than 50 percent of all species of life on earth. Without their natural habitat, those species would perish.

The largest and best-known tropical rain forest fills a vast region of the Amazon River basin in Brazil. Its evolution has taken millions of years. It is so complex that it is more than a single habitat where certain creatures and plants live on the ground and others live in the trees. It is many-tiered, with each layer filled with life that is unique to that layer alone. Think of a skyscraper where each floor houses different people speaking different languages and doing and making different things, all without much awareness of what is going on on the floors above or below. They would be mutually sustained by the water pipes, electricity lines, and elevators that serve every floor, but on each

In Brazil, the Amazon Highway brings land
exploitation into the jungle. In this
particular area of the Brazilian rain forest,
the clear-cut area is adjacent to an area
that will be left untouched.

floor life would be self-contained. Chop down a 200-foot-tall (60 m) tree in a rain forest and more than the monkey at its top will hit the ground.

Brazil is a giant country, larger than the United States. Like the United States about 100 years ago, Brazil is expanding into its interior. For the settler in the U.S., the land rush was to the open spaces of the plains and the great West. In Brazil, settlers and others are flocking into the rain forest. The pioneer in America plowed the soil to farm the land, but in the rain forests the trees have to go first. Since the 1970s, about 20 percent of the Brazilian rain forest has been destroyed. It can never be replaced. If the destruction continues at the rate it is today, the entire forest will be gone in twenty-five years. That's about how long it would take for someone born today to grow up, graduate from college, and get started in a career.

Less than 5 percent of earth's rain forests are presently protected from exploitation. The rest, it seems, and all the life in them, is doomed.

Other kinds of forests are also being destroyed. The timberlands of the American West are falling to loggers. On the island of Madagascar off the east coast of Africa, over 90 percent of plant life has already disappeared. And on the skirts of the Himalayan Mountains between Asia and the Indian subcontinent, once forested hills have been clipped away so that they can no longer hold back the heavy monsoon rains that drench them each year. Floods race over the lowlands below them in man-made disasters that have killed thousands of people.

Sicily, the large island just off the pointed "toe"

of Italy, was once covered with dense forests. Two thousand years ago, Greek mariners, and later others who settled its rich lands, cut the trees for fuel and building and to make ships. Today, all the trees in Sicily gathered in one place would not make a very impressive state park compared to what it once was.

There are trees in the United States that are 1,000 years old. They survive in scattered sections of ancient forests that used to blanket large areas of the North American continent. All but about 15 percent of the original forests are gone. Some of them will remain because they are in protected national parks and wildlife preserves, but the rest could go the way of Sicily's, or Brazil's, or Madagascar's, and all the other forests that are being shaved off the earth in as few as fifteen years and probably no more than fifty.

# 3
# AIR POLLUTION

The Industrial Revolution and the 200 years of factories it spawned are easy to blame for the increase in carbon dioxide and other pollutants that fill the atmosphere. It would follow that since industry made the air dirty in the first place, industry should clean it up. Find the factories that make the smoke, force them to stop, and the battle for clean air would be won. But it isn't the factories that do the most polluting. Only 15 percent of smog, a smelly mix of airborne chemicals and by-products of combustion, come from industry. Over twice that—40 percent—comes from places like bakeries, dry cleaning plants, and consumer items (we've already mentioned spray cans). Another 40 percent comes from vehicle exhaust, which includes other toxic materials as well.

Just about everyone is responsible for polluting the air. Even the innocent act of burning wood in a fireplace adds pollutants and more carbon dioxide to the air. One fireplace doesn't add much pollution any more than one car does. It might smell strong close up, but by the time the wind gets a grip on the smoke and scatters it around, there isn't enough left to make your eyes water. But a thousand fireplaces in a mountain valley can fill the valley. Tens of millions of cars do far, far worse.

## Air Quality

The dangers of polluted air aren't at all invisible. In Greece, ancient temples and statuary that has braved thousands of years of ordinary weather are being eaten away by the twentieth century's potent air. In Germany, the famed Black Forest is dying because of acid rain, which is nothing more than air pollution dissolved in water. If Germany or Greece seem too far away as an example, take the time to watch the sunset. In many parts of the United States, the western sky now fills with vivid colors that were not there in the past when the sun went down. Like an invisible prism, microscopically thin clouds of chemicals refract sunlight to turn dusk into a tapestry of hues beautiful to see but frightening when their cause is understood.

If it were possible to mine the air, fortunes in chemicals could be recovered. In 1985, a Californian environmentalist and congressman estimated that U.S. industry and other sources pumped about 80 million pounds (36 million kg) of toxic chemicals into the air *every year.* That's 20,000 tons, or about half the weight of the U.S.S. *Iowa,* America's largest battleship. If 1,000 BBs (shot pellets) weigh

1 pound, that would be 80 billion BBs. If they were scattered evenly over the entire United States, only about 8,500 BBs would land on every square mile (2.6 sq km). Every year. You might not find one the first year, but the odds would double the next year. If you lived to be 100, there would be 850,000 BBs on every square mile. They would be a lot easier to find.

However, when a law was passed that made corporations reveal how much toxic pollution they actually put into the air, it was discovered that thirty-four times the estimated amount went up with the smoke and other emissions from plants and factories. In BBs, that would mean there would be about 290,000 on each square mile of the U.S. in the first year. One hundred years later, there would be 29 million. The ground wouldn't exactly be slippery, but you would definitely notice them on picnics.

Airborne pollutants aren't BBs. They are chemical compounds. Mix a BB in water and nothing happens. Mix sulfur dioxide ($SO_2$) with water and you get sulfuric acid, a potent chemical that can dissolve stone. Sulfur dioxide is only one of many toxic pollutants you see in the sunset. It doesn't stay in the sky, of course. Dissolved in water that has been carried aloft in the continuous recycling of that natural resource, it falls to the ground as acid rain.

## Toxic Air

There is more in the air you breathe than oxygen, nitrogen, carbon dioxide, and an occasional puff of smoke, a few grains of plant pollen, a whiff of wet leaves, or a sneeze of dust. There is sulfuric acid, too, as we have just seen—but that's not the worst of it.

For example, over the past two decades scientists have detected chemical compounds in fish caught in Lake Superior. The lake, almost as big as Indiana, conjures up images of Native Americans canoeing over a crystal surface of water clear enough to drink. Once upon a time, you *could* drink the water. But no more. What puzzled the scientists was that the chemicals should not have been in the fish because they should not have been in the water. There was no explanation for how chemical compounds such as PCBs, DDT, and toxaphene, a chlorinated hydrocarbon insecticide, found their way into the "sky-blue waters" of Lake Superior. There were no known sources from which the wastes could enter. Yet, as countless affected fish, birds, and other wildlife in and near the lake attested, the stuff was there.

For example, fish were found with close to the "allowed" limit of DDT in their flesh. Birds with fatal birth defects that prevented them from eating or standing were hatching. Creatures like mink and river otters were vanishing. And the nesting population of bald eagles, an American symbol of wilderness purity, was thinning, probably because they were eating gulls tainted with toxic chemicals. Humans—babies with low birth weights, abnormal reflexes, and other problems—were also suspected victims of the unexplained toxins in the water.

Nobody knew where the harmful chemicals, particularly the toxaphene, were coming from. The

Canadian government strictly controlled the use of toxaphene. In the U.S. the nearest likely sources—and they were so far away they didn't seem likely at all—were California and the Southern cotton-growing states. Toxaphene was used to control the boll weevil, the perennial pest that destroys millions of dollars' worth of cotton each year—but in the cotton belt of the Deep South, not in the grain belt of the northern plains. So how did chemicals intended to kill a tiny pest in North Carolina or Mississippi get into the food chain in Minnesota and Michigan?

Scientists began to probe the air and bodies of water, moving their tests north from the cotton fields, where they suspected the material originated, to Lake Superior. Their conclusions were startling. Chlorinated hydrocarbons, which were previously believed to be transferred from soil to streams, rivers, and lakes by runoff water, were also being transported in twentieth-century fashion—they were flying.

Toxaphene was being lofted into the air from fields where it was sprayed to fight weevils, and was floating through the air on the wings of the wind, reaching not only Lake Superior, but also the air over the Atlantic Ocean, lakes in Sweden, the North Sea, and the Alps, and even Antarctica.

Other chemicals floating in the air fall to the ground with the rain, and eventually wind up in the human food chain. Sixteen different trace metals, including lead, zinc, cadmium, and copper have been studied. One conclusion is that more toxic metals enter the air every year than do radioactive and organic pollutants combined.

When the volcano Krakatoa erupted in 1883, powdery ash and dust traveled around the world in the stratosphere for over two years. Brilliant sunsets caused by the natural airborne pollutants were reported from all over the world. The material eventually settled to earth. Man-made airborne pollutants are no different. What goes up does, indeed, come down—wherever the winds decide.

Wind is moving air, and air is the breath of life. When alien matter—whether oily auto emissions, excess carbon dioxide, ozone-destroying aerosol propellants, sulfur-laden smoke, or insecticide-laced wind—enters the atmosphere—someone or something living somewhere on the planet is going to eat it, breathe it, or feel its effects, now, tomorrow, or in the future.

## Acid Rain

Raindrops have always been a symbol of purity. Soap ads and poetry are sprinkled with fresh water, bubbling brooks, and sparkling clear lakes. Unfortunately, much of the earth's water now has something besides fish in it.

Acid rain is produced when the by-products of fossil fuel combustion combine with atmospheric water. Smoke from smokestacks that sometimes tower 1,000 feet (305 m) in the air is laden with sulfur dioxide, nitrogen oxides, and other chemicals. Wind and weather carry the smoke through the sky, often hundreds of miles away from where it was generated. The chemical-filled air becomes saturated with evaporated moisture lifted from the ground, and clouds are formed. When the clouds become supersaturated with water the water condenses into drops which fall to the ground as rain. Unlike the pure water that went into the sky, the rainwater is now laden with chemicals.

Each time an acid rain cloud drops its lethal load, the earth below takes a chemical bath. Over time, the chemicals in the soil accumulate until they are strong enough to affect whatever grows on that soil. When the pollution becomes strong enough to kill plants and trees, the local environment is changed. As we saw, when an environment changes, everything living in it—from insects to higher animals, including humans—suffers the consequences.

The deadly by-products of faraway factories do not stop in the dirt of the forest floor. Soil is only a sponge, not a bucket. Water runs through it easily, urged downhill by gravity, constantly flowing toward the sea. The water that does not soak into the ground runs off into streams, lakes, and rivers. The underground water also moves, tugged by the same natural forces. Whatever the water touches becomes tainted by chemicals formed when ancient fossil fuels—mostly coal high in sulfur—were burned to make energy.

The main sources of sulfur dioxide in the United States are fifty high-sulfur-coal–burning electricity-generating plants scattered mostly through the Midwest. They alone produce about half of all the sulfur dioxide in this country. There are many similar generating stations and coal-fired factories around the world, and their effects are disastrous.

In Hungary, it is estimated that one of every seventeen people who die are killed by air pollu-

*The United States is not alone in its air pollution problems. Copsa Mica, Romania, a city with severe air pollution problems, is only one of many cities in eastern Europe now addressing its environmental catastrophes.*

tion. The Soviet Union admits that its pollution problems are catastrophic. Compelling circumstantial evidence shows that in the eastern U.S. and Canada, where natural weather patterns carry much of U.S.-produced acid rain, human cancers and death have increased. In the tropics and subarctic, entire species of plant and animal life are threatened. Lakes, rivers, and coastal bays are twice-hit, first by acidified water and second by the algae that grows when acid levels rise. As many as 14,000 lakes in Canada are so acidified that their native fish have died off. Of the lakes in the Adirondack Mountains, 25 percent are too acidic to support fish. Chesapeake Bay, the United States' largest estuary, has been severely polluted by nitrogen compounds, which, like sulfur dioxide, are byproducts of fossil fuel combustion.

Not everyone agrees that acid rain is the cause of all this destruction. And there is evidence that lake acidification is not as rapid as had been predicted, possibly because of laws that have restricted sulfur dioxide emissions. But small gains cannot erase the very real fact that acid rain is a major environmental threat.

# 4
# WATER POLLUTION

In 1985, a young merchant-marine cadet peered over the side of the ship carrying him and 900 fellow cadets on their annual training cruise across the Atlantic Ocean to Europe. As the giant converted ocean liner plowed through the water, the cadet noticed a strange assortment of floating trash lying off the ship's bow. Most was forgettable debris—plastic, glass bottles, chunks of Styrofoam, and other durable junk. But standing out like biscuits in a bowl of soup were countless worn-out bunk-bed mattresses. The ship passed them by and they were forgotten.

Three weeks later, as the ship retraced its course back to New York, the same cadet was on the bridge when the island of floating trash appeared once again. The very same mattresses, still buoyed by summer waves, flopped soggily by and for a second time disappeared over the horizon.

The cadet shook his head. That night he wrote in his journal, "What you throw into the ocean stays in the ocean."

Very little new water is being added to earth's supply through volcanic action and other natural phenomena. What's here has been here from the very beginning. Much of what is put into it will stay, perhaps to the very end.

How the mattresses ended up in the sea is a mystery. How much of the other pollution that pours into the ocean every year gets there is not. There are over 2,000 major municipal and industrial treatment plants dumping wastes into the waters of America every year. Ocean shipping adds another 6 million metric tons. Nobody knows the total amount of garbage, spilled oil, chemical wastes, raw sewage, sludge, and other pollutants that find their way into the sea, or where most of it comes from.

## Water Quality

America has approximately 3.5 million miles (5.6 million km) of rivers and streams. Less than 10,000 of them are protected by the nation's Wild Scenic River System laws. The rest, plus tens of thousands of lakes, ponds, and other bodies of open water, large and small, are under assault.

The Environmental Protection Agency estimates that 42 million Americans may be drinking water containing unsafe levels of lead, a toxic metal. About 1,000 other contaminants have been detected in public water supplies. Twenty percent of America's public water supplies contain industrial chemicals.

Even bottled water may contain chemical solvents, pesticides, heavy metals, and bacteria.

Water pollution comes from three general sources. One is acid rain. The others originate on land from either a "point source," which is a specific, identifiable location such as a sewage treatment plant, or a "nonpoint source," which has no precise point of entry. Runoff from agricultural areas that have been doused with pesticides is pollution from a nonpoint source. The main nonpoint sources of pollution are urban areas, farms, construction sites, mines, and logging operations. Nonpoint pollution sources are hard to control because they are hard to find.

Fish are among the first creatures to suffer the effects of polluted water. A sampling of fish taken from the Great Lakes found that nine of every ten fish contained unsafe levels of toxic substances such as PCBs, DDT, dieldrin, mirex, chlordane, toxaphene, and mercury.

Other marine dwellers, large and small, are hit by water pollution. Dolphins have died off the Atlantic coast of the United States, mussels have been poisoned in the Canadian Maritime Provinces, and the long-spined black sea urchin that inhabits the Caribbean and the waters off Florida and the Bahamas is nearly extinct.

Ocean pollution has reached critical proportions according to some marine biologists and environmentalists. Most coastal pollution comes from land-based sources, the final resting place of the chemicals, acid rain, and agricultural runoff that is born far inland in cities, farms, and forests. Dramatic events like massive oil spills grip the public's attention. Their visible damage, like their cause, is obvious. The disaster created by the giant tanker the *Exxon Valdez*, off the Alaskan coast in the spring of 1989 riveted viewers to television screens for weeks. Its effects will take decades to overcome, and some things will never be the same. But hidden sources of pollution that lie along distant waterways are just as deadly. Industrial waste, sewage, and agricultural pollution worry the experts as much as do oil spills.

Toxic material in the water kills life, but not all pollution is toxic. Nitrogen, for example, supports plant life, and nitrogen by-products of fossil-fuel burning are carried in acid rain. Nitrogen is also found in agricultural runoff. Excessive amounts of these materials in waterways, bays, or coastal areas nourish the algae normally growing there, resulting in an algae "bloom," an explosive growth of algae that takes over the water it lives in, suffocating everything else. When that happens, all that is left is murky water loaded with poison and slime.

Ocean water was never drinkable. But lake, stream, and spring water were this country's original sources of drinking water. Dug wells, where a wooden bucket lowered into the cold depths of clear underground water was hauled up by hand and its sparkling contents sipped from a tin dipper, came next. As the demand for wells grew, drilled wells were pierced far into the ground to tap water from subterranean streams or vast aquifers. Towns and cities built systems that gathered water from lakes, reservoirs, or rivers and purified it before piping it into homes for daily use. Now many fresh-

*Oil spills are responsible for long-term damage to the environment. Here, a cleanup crew doing shore washing at Prince William Sound is attempting to undo some of the catastrophic damage done by the Exxon Valdez oil spill.*

water sources are suspect—possible carriers of pollutants that harm.

Chronic, or long-term, exposure to toxic materials can be harmful to humans—and other animal life—in a number of ways. Some toxic materials produce heart, circulatory system, nervous system, and immune system damage that takes many years to appear. Some toxic materials are carcinogenic (cancer-causing), some are mutagenic (they change the cell's genetic code), and some are taratogenic ("monster-causing", that is, they injure an embryo or fetus so that the human or other animal offspring suffers birth defects).

The Environmental Protection Agency (EPA) states that there are 700 identifiable chemicals found in U.S. drinking water. This agency adds that 129 of these are dangerous. Most water-treatment plants don't have the equipment to test for them or to filter them out. Consequently, they end up in America's water supply. About 30 toxic substances have been proven to be carcinogenic, but as many as 200 others may be. Some of the thirty, like arsenic, benzene, and vinyl chloride, are common in drinking water.

Pollutants enter the water supply through a variety of ways. Some occur naturally by leaching into groundwater or deep aquifers from the surrounding soil or rock. Uranium, radon, radium, flu-

*Agricultural runoff, if the soil has been permeated with pesticides, is one of the main sources of water pollution.*

59

oride, salt, and elemental metals (aluminum, copper, silver, zinc, and others) are examples. Most pollutants, however, are human-made or are the chemical by-products of human-made substances, and get into the drinking water because they are put there, either directly or indirectly.

For example, rain- and irrigation water absorb and suspend chemical substances as they wash over the ground and soak through the soil. Water that does not evaporate back into the atmosphere runs off or through the ground and carries whatever is in it to streams, rivers, and lakes, or soaks deep into aquifers.

Some pollutants enter the water-supply system directly because they are put there to purify the water. Chlorine is perhaps the best known of these. Other pollutants are formed by chemical reactions among chemicals and other impurities in the water. Still others get into the water as it goes through the system's pipes. Lead from lead pipes or from soldered joints in copper pipe, and asbestos from asbestos cement pipes are examples.

Industrial and agricultural pollutants are the most widespread and potentially harmful of the toxic materials found in drinking water. The tongue-twisting lexicon of industrial chemicals includes acetaldehyde, bromobenzene, dichlorobenzene, dichlorodifluoromethane, nitrobenzene, styrene, trichlorethane, vinyl chloride, and xylene. Agricultural pesticides—and there are almost 50,000 of them—are no easier on the tongue, to say or to taste. They include alachlor, chlordane, dichloro-phenoxyacetic acid, dichloro-diphenyl-trichloro-ethane (DDT), and toxaphene. Industrial wastes may

60

be discharged as factory waste into rivers, may escape from containers thought to be sealed, or may be illegally dumped. Some may be washed out of mining tailings or factory dump sites by rain. Agricultural pesticides leach into groundwater or are flushed away with irrigation or rain runoff.

Water pollution is virtually everywhere. From underground aquifers, surface rivers and lakes, and airborne rain to the final destination of all water, the ocean—which is also water's source—the creeping stain of pollution threatens to change nature's life-giving liquid into a deadly broth.

The maritime cadet's observation about ocean trash can be extended to water everywhere. What you put into the water, any water, anywhere, stays there.

# 5
# WASTE DISPOSAL

Archaeologists who study ancient cultures strike historical "gold" whenever they come upon a dump site that was used by the people they are examining. By analyzing primitive stone axes and flint arrowheads or broken bits of pottery and petrified pieces of leather, they are able to write chapters about the lives that were lived nearby, scores, hundreds, or thousands of years ago. Even today an abandoned dump behind an old farmhouse or a pile of rubbish at a little-used edge of town reveals much about the people who put it there. If an ancient site or old dump is not handy, look in your own basement, attic, or garage, or even into the back of your closet. The story will be the same— people throw away lots of things.

There are two enduring mysteries in American life. One is: Where did the other sock disappear to? The second is: How does one bag of groceries make two bags of garbage? The answer to the first, like the missing sock, will never be found. The answer to the second is equally perplexing. What happens to the two bags of garbage is not.

The average American household produces about 6¾ bags of garbage every week, or about 650 bags a year. Added to the rest of the annual waste dumped in America, it would fill a trash container as big as a football field with sides 30,000 feet (9,150 m) tall. Mt. Everest, the world's tallest mountain, is 29,000 feet (8,845 m) tall.

There is no such trash can, of course. And even if there were, where would we put it? That's the question most on the minds of trash experts as they try to figure out where to put the garbage itself.

Most of the places used to dump trash in the past will be filled and closed by 1995. It is illegal to dump garbage into the ocean. Burning it in large incinerators is expensive and not yet environmentally acceptable. Some, like the bottles and cans you return to the store, is recycled, but most—about 90 percent—stays trash. Nobody wants a garbage dump in their backyard, and nobody wants to pay the increasing costs to carry trash away to places where it still can be dumped legally. Now add this harrowing fact: the amount of garbage we generate will have doubled between the years 1960 and 2000 at its present rate. We are already 80 percent there.

On a state-by-state basis, many less populated parts of the country won't have to worry about their dumps being full for more than ten years. Others have up to ten years to think about the problem, but a number of eastern states will have to find solutions in less than five years. Ten years is hardly more time for complacency than under five is. There are refrigerators guaranteed to last that long. No matter which state they finally "die" in, there will be no place to hold the funeral because most landfills will be full.

Most American waste is paper, not refrigerators. About 50 percent of the nation's trash is newspapers, junk mail, old phone books, the wrapping from thousands of products from the supermarket, computer printouts, and paper of every imaginable kind. Metal, glass, plastic, organic kitchen waste, wood, yard waste (leaves, grass cuttings, trees, and branches), and toxic wastes make up the rest.

Recycling was thought to be the solution to the sea of garbage. By returning aluminum cans and glass and plastic bottles, the materials used in their manufacture could be used over again, often at great savings. In addition, raw natural resources could be left alone until they were really needed. Paper also has a second and a third life. By grinding paper back into pulp, trees could be saved, costs could be cut, and everyone would have the satisfaction of helping to manage waste. Even the plastic foam containers used by fast-food outlets to keep burgers and fries warm can be turned back into new products. Recycling was something people could do something about right in their own kitchens and garages, places that are much closer than Alaskan oil spills or holes in the ozone layer.

But there has already been more old paper collected than can be used within the foreseeable future, and only 10 percent of old glass finds its

way back to recycled products. Aluminum cans have a higher success rate because they are ten times cheaper than aluminum processed from raw ore. Still, only about 50 percent of the cans that leave supermarkets and vending machines are returned. Plastic does much worse. Only 1 pound (0.45 kg) out of 100 (45 kg) is recycled.

Luckily, as science and industry continue to develop new uses for recycled material, their value will increase. Whether enough products using recycled materials can be invented before the waste they would be made from buries us is another question.

Some material can never be recycled. Instead it has to be disposed of permanently.

## Hazardous Waste

When arrowheads were chipped from flint as weapons, the flakes fell to the ground and were left there. Some can still be found in the woodlands and prairies where Native Americans roamed as recently as the end of the nineteenth century. Other, far older sites also remain undisturbed, perhaps to be discovered by future hikers or scientists bent on finding traces of the past.

*Recycling centers throughout the country, such as this one in Danbury, Connecticut, are attempting to do something about the overwhelming amount of garbage we generate.*

67

Today when weapons and virtually anything else are made, their by-products are not as benign as a flint chip. Some are even deadly. If America has a waste-disposal problem with its household garbage, and it does, then what is it to do with wastes that kill?

The record has not been very good so far. As recently as the 1970s, hazardous chemical wastes were being poured directly into holes in the ground. Where they have seeped to by now defies the imagination, although the presence of chemicals in drinking water probably accounts for some of them.

Other wastes were placed in steel drums which were sometimes sealed and sometimes not and were buried under a layer of soil thick enough to cover them. The sites were easily forgotten. Some may never be found. Others, such as the infamous Love Canal site, were found, but by the time the 22,000 tons of chemicals buried beneath a schoolyard in the quiet upstate New York community were discovered, it was too late. For years people had lived innocently on top of a poisonous stew that leached toxins through the soil of their neighborhood into their air, their water, and eventually, even into their bones.

Today's disposal techniques are an improvement. Rather than open pits or thinly covered sites, hazardous wastes are buried in special holes in the ground called *cells.* The bottom of the cell is made of hard-packed clay and is lined with huge sheets of plastic. Someone who did not know what it is might think the hole is a vast open-pit mine. Bulldozers and earthmovers are dwarfed by their size.

*Sealed steel drums, locked behind gates at a manufacturing plant, are an attempt to safely confine hazardous waste.*

Chemical and other hazardous wastes that cannot be disposed of normally in ordinary landfills, or by incineration or other means, are mixed with a kind of cement and put into 55-gallon drums. The drums are sealed and are placed in the cell. After the cell has been filled, it is covered with clay. Another plastic liner is sealed over the top, creating a giant plastic "baggie" which is covered with ordinary soil and is then landscaped. A pumping system draws off the water that collects inside the cell, and the water is then disposed of safely. The cells are designed to last forever, so accurate records of each cell are kept. Hundreds of years from now, people will know what lies beneath an otherwise innocent-looking piece of land.

Most hazardous waste never reaches a cell-type disposal facility. Only about 4 percent of hazardous-waste disposal is as efficient or as long-lasting. Fewer then twenty years ago, hazardous wastes were often dumped into open holes to soak into the raw earth. Now most is disposed of at the plant or factory where it was generated.

## Infectious Waste

A particularly nasty kind of waste is the medical waste generated by hospitals, doctors' offices, and health-care facilities such as nursing homes. Also called infectious waste, although not all of it is capable of causing disease, it is an assortment of potentially hazardous trash that must be disposed of with special treatment and care. Unfortunately, not all of it is handled the way it should be.

Infectious waste, also called "red-bag" waste for the special containers it is supposed to be placed in for disposal, has been a by-product of health care for years. In the summer of 1988 this waste-disposal problem received national attention. The closing of a number of eastern seaboard beaches from New Jersey to Massachusetts brought the ugly mess to the front pages. Numerous used hypodermic syringes and needles, vials of blood, and other medical trash from unknown sources washed up on popular bathing beaches. Officials were forced to close the beaches to the public, fearing that unwary swimmers and sunbathers might be infected by contact with the potentially dangerous stuff. Vials of blood, for example, thought to be samples drawn for medical tests and then discarded, were found to contain AIDS antibodies and the hepatitis B virus.

Some researchers maintain that catching AIDS from medical waste is unlikely because even in fresh blood it is highly diluted and dies quickly when exposed to the environment. The danger of becoming ill from hepatitis B virus is greater because it can remain infectious for weeks.

Experts in waste management estimate that as much as 500,000 tons of infectious wastes are produced in the United States every year. New York State alone, with its large population and many medical facilities, is said to generate as much as 125 tons a day.

Not all medical waste is disposed of in the sea, of course, and not much of that actually reaches the shore. Perhaps no more than 1 to 10 percent found on beaches in the summer of 1988 was medical waste. Most trash that ruins beaches is the ordinary stuff, every bit as ugly, but at least not so deadly. A combination of events led to the problems on New York beaches. Some of the waste that washed up is suspected of having been dumped into the sea by dishonest haulers who would otherwise have had to pay to dispose of it in approved facilities. It is also believed that some health-care facilities may have illegally dumped their trash into the ocean to avoid having to pay the high cost of having it hauled away properly. Some of the medical waste may have spilled from barges transporting it and other garbage to a deep-ocean dump site. Unusual wind patterns pushed this floating material to shore. Ordinarily it would have been blown out to sea.

Ideally, infectious waste should be incinerated at high temperatures. Thirty-two states require that it be disinfected. Presently, however, available technology and services to properly dispose of it are unable to meet the demand. Some companies are developing methods to dispose of medical waste. One way is to grind it up and disinfect it with chlorine, the same chemical used to purify municipal water supplies. Another is to burn waste in special high-temperature incinerators that limit the amount of pollution put into the air. Laws enforcing approved methods of disposal of medical waste will tighten controls on how such material is handled, but as long as people willfully break laws, the laws will be ineffective unless they are backed up by strict enforcement.

# 6
# TOXIC COPS

The consequences of pollution are enormous and far-flung. Pollution fills our ecosphere from the floor of the sea to the edge of the atmosphere, finally ending in the wispy, ozone-bearing reaches that border outer space. That is where it ends, but not where it began. The culprits, of course, are people.

But people are also its victims. The dangers to the environment and all living things reviewed in this book did not happen naturally. They are the direct or indirect result of the activities of only one of the millions of life-forms dependent for survival on the very thing they—we—are destroying: the delicate balance of billions of years of evolution. That one, most responsible life form is people.

Although everyone must share some of the responsibility for the problems of pollution, some are more guilty than others. And, if the balance of nature is to be restored, everyone must bear some of the burden to end willful polluting. Some have already accepted a far greater share of the burden. They are the "Toxic Cops."

## "Johnny Cash" on Garbage Mountain

Staten Island is a borough of the city of New York, but it nestles against the state of New Jersey like a child clinging to its mother. It is a true island, bordered on all sides by water. Its links to the mainland are human-made. Four huge bridges of concrete and steel span two riverlike channels, or "kills," and the Narrows, a much broader channel that connects New York Harbor to the Atlantic Ocean. Three join the island to New Jersey, and the fourth, the towering Verrazano Narrows suspension bridge, unites it with Brooklyn, another of the five New York City boroughs. At night all five boroughs sparkle with lights, but there are fewer lights on Staten Island, and some large areas show no light at all. Tucked away in uninhabited places, the darkened regions are as remote as Staten Island itself. For almost seven years of dark nights, one such area, New York City's Brookfield landfill in a dark corner of Staten Island, was the scene of an ongoing crime.

A number of landfills are situated around New York City to handle the 30,000 tons of waste it generates daily. One, the Fresh Kills landfill, is the largest dump on earth. The landfills rise from the ground like giant boils of seething garbage during the day. At night they are virtually invisible. A driver

*This sea of garbage, complete with sea
gulls flying overhead, is the site of the
Fresh Kills landfill on Staten Island,
New York, the largest dump on earth.*

passing by on a roadway would not see them if they didn't block out big patches of stars, and even then they blend into the darkness of night. The smell, however, is inescapable. Gases from the decomposing garbage constantly rise through the muck and drift like mischievous campfire smoke, always blowing into your face.

One moonless night in 1976, a tanker truck that could have been mistaken for a fuel-oil transport pulled away from the back of a manufacturing plant in Brooklyn and headed west. It threaded its way down quiet city streets lined with cars. During the day the streets would be full of life, but this late at night they and the surrounding neighborhoods were quiet.

The truck reached the approach to the Verrazano-Narrows Bridge. The driver had made this trip many times and knew the route well. He did not have to rely on the green billboards marking Interstate Highway 278, the roadway that begins in the Bronx as the Bruckner Expressway, changes its name to the Brooklyn-Queens Expressway, and then turns into a bridge to span the nation's busiest harbor. Once it touched down on Staten Island, the highway would become the Staten Island Expressway before crossing one more bridge and coming to an end on the New Jersey side. The truck would not go that far. Its destination was the Brookfield landfill.

The bridge hung like a necklace over the black water, lighted from end to end by brilliant floodlamps that turned its eight-lane deck into daylight. The truck driver paid the bridge toll and nursed his rig onto the span. He glanced out the passenger side window as the truck neared the center of the bridge. A number of ships lay at anchor in the harbor, and in the distance, Manhattan, the jewel of the five boroughs, twinkled its lights from skyscraping buildings that rose to blend with the stars. The truck made an unholy noise for such a serene time and place, bellowing angrily between shifts as it climbed the sloping rise to the top and then speeded down the other side.

Cruising deep into Staten Island, the driver turned on to smaller and smaller roadways until he found his destination. The Brookfield landfill, like its festering cousins scattered around New York City, hung in a squat heap under the cover of darkness. The truck entered the gate. It rumbled over the man-made garbage hill to a place nobody could see even in broad daylight and stopped. The driver leaped from the cab and stepped to the rear of the tanker. Unlike most criminals in the commission of their crime, he showed no fear. What he was about to do had been going on for four years and would continue for another three years before criminals and justice collided head on. He raised his hand to the tanker's side and turned a valve handle.

The driver stood back. A gush of foul-smelling chemicals spurted from the back of the tanker onto the ground. The stream was as thick as the driver's arm at first and then grew smaller as its power was spent. When it stopped, the driver closed the valve and returned to the truck's cab. The puddle of black goo on the ground spread to the size of a small pond as it slowly seeped into the garbage below. Eventually some of it would leach into deep underground water supplies, and some would reach the sea.

The landfill was not unattended. Strict controls governed what could be dumped at the site. The job of managing the dump was the responsibility of the New York City Department of Sanitation. A night supervisor at Brookfield, John Cassiliano, was known to the driver of the tanker rig simply as "Johnny Cash." For good reason.

From 1972 until 1979, "Johnny Cash" allowed illegal nighttime dumping of chemical wastes at Brookfield by unscrupulous private haulers. In return for what was estimated at a total of more than $600,000 in payoffs for the privilege, Cassiliano permitted toxic materials to be drained into the garbage mountain the city of New York paid him to protect. Caught and convicted, he was imprisoned in 1982 for his crimes. The Department of Sanitation was stunned and embarrassed by the scandal that followed.

## Environmental Police Unit

The stinging realization that one of its own had betrayed the city prompted the organization of a new kind of unit within the Department of Sanitation. The word went out that a team of detectives would be recruited and trained to deal with environmental lawbreakers. It would be called the Environmental Police (EP) unit and would consist of a small core of determined detectives and their supervisors whose job it would be to track down illegal polluters, and bring them to justice. The unit would be armed with legal statutes, and, to under-score the danger they might face when confront-ing people who flagrantly disregarded the rights and safety of others, they would also pack snugly fitting .38-caliber Smith & Wesson pistols. They would be real police in every way. But a significant difference from ordinary Police Department officer candidates resulted from the requirement that san-itation police officers have two years experience in the Department of Sanitation.

A team of thirteen men was formed in Novem-ber 1984. Headed by a lawyer, Daniel Millstone, the group consisted of two lieutenants and ten de-tectives. They became the nation's first full-time en-vironmental law enforcement officers, or "environ-mental police."

The force has grown to twenty-two people. At times twice that number could be used. A half dozen attorneys share the legal load with Millstone. Their conviction rate is over 95 percent. The unit is equipped with cars, radios, tape recorders, video recorders, and even a boat. A public relations per-son works closely with area hospitals.

In the fateful summer of 1988, before dirty needles began to wash ashore like the broken spines of a metal sea urchin, the EP unit fielded two dozen calls a day from people reporting sus-pected acts of pollution. When the wind shifted toward the beaches rather than blowing out to sea, spilled debris began to dot the sand. The unit's telephones screamed as a hundred calls a day poured in. Bags of needles, bits of glass, and small vials of a dark substance—blood—were being found with frightening regularity up and down a hundred miles (160 km) of coastal shore. Bathers and waders avoided their usual summertime haunts, afraid that a misstep might result in a scratch from a broken vial or a miniature stabbing by a deadly needle.

Regardless of the small statistical possibility of contracting a disease from the trash, nobody wanted to swim in it or lie on the sand next to it. Who would? AIDS and hepatitis are deadly illnesses. The discovery of fewer than 3,000 needles from New York City beaches was enough to hold millions of beachgoers hostage, even though only one of the city's seventy-four hospitals alone, Bellevue, uses a thousand times that many—3 million—a year. The odds of being stuck, much less even finding one, were lower than the chances of being hit by lightning. But nobody wanted to take the chance. Warned of the seaborne trash on their beaches by front-page newspaper headlines, bathers stayed away in droves. The cost in lost business at seashore establishments was as high as $2 billion.

The scare died away with the season, but the memory of what might lurk beneath the inviting waters of the Atlantic Ocean did not. Needles in the sea were more real than *Jaws*. The fanciful movie monster had cleared the beaches of a make-believe Long Island resort town, but people flocked back for the next episode. Nobody who enjoys the real ocean can visit it now without remembering the real scare of the summer of '88.

The EP was not a sleeping giant waiting for the events of '88 to awaken it to action. From its for-

*Members of the New York City Department of Sanitation Environmental Police Unit, in protective garb, examine waste disposed at an undisclosed waste disposal site for possible hazardous, infectious, or asbestos material.*

mation in 1984 to the present, the unit has been and remains on twenty-four-hour call. Most of what it does does not make headlines. A lot of it should.

## The Bribe

September. Bone-chilling winter weather was still a few months away, but summer was definitely over. The common three- and four-story brick apartment buildings lining the streets of the Bronx continued to bask under the final rays of an Indian-summer sun, but landlords and residents knew from experience how quickly heat turns to cold in New York City. Oil heat, lots of it, would be needed soon. Now was the time to repair broken boilers and their fittings.

Jailal Jagmohan knew repairs would be needed in the boiler room of the apartment building he owned on Kingsbridge Road. He ordered work to begin. Repairmen began the task by stripping the maze of pipes in the musty basement room of its protective insulation. The material was dusty, and pieces of it flaked away when it was torn from the pipes. Small and large bits dropped to the floor. The big chunks were stuffed into green plastic garbage bags. A dozen bags were soon filled. Rather than leave them piled on the floor where they were in the way, the workers hauled the bags up a short flight of concrete stairs and stacked them willy-nilly on the sidewalk near the curb. There were 30,000 tons of New York City garbage waiting to be collected on that September 30. The twelve bags from Jagmohan's basement didn't look much different and would have made no difference had they been at the curb or not. But what was inside would turn Jagmohan's world upside down.

A New York City Sanitation Department truck wheezed to a stop in front of the bags piled outside 235 Kingsbridge Road. Its engine rumbled noisily as a sanitation man stepped to the stack of loosely tied green sacks, ready to flip them into the truck's hopper as he'd done with thousands of identical bags before. They would end up buried in one of the city's landfills by nightfall. The next day the truck would be back for more. But something about the bags stood out. These bags were different. The sanitation man left the bags where they were. Suspecting what they contained, he notified authorities.

Rocco Siclari was glad it was Friday when he arrived for work at 253 Broadway in lower Manhattan that morning. The summer had been filled with endless days of investigating the flood of infectious-waste pollution that had closed the city's beaches. Things had quieted down, but even so, Rocco looked forward to the weekend.

He entered the lobby of the tall granite office building. Once the home of an insurance company whose name was still inscribed in stone above the door, the building was now filled with New York City employees. He passed the unmanned security-guard desk in the lobby and walked to the bank of elevators, joining others who were also arriving for work.

Siclari, who stands 6 feet, 5 inches (195.6 cm) tall and weighs 40 pounds (18 kg) per foot, stepped from the elevator at the eighth floor and walked to Room 800, a suite of offices housing New York

83

City's Department of Sanitation Environmental Police Unit. His desk, like those of his fellow officers, was in the largest room, just off the unit's small reception area. Rocco glanced at a colorful poster on the wall, the only decoration in the drab anteroom. It showed a full-sailed yacht plowing a furrow of white water through a deep-green sea. He smiled at the receptionist tapping away at a computer console. "If that was taken off Staten Island this summer, I hope nobody fell overboard," he said, admiring the tanned crew struggling to keep the boat upright. He knew there was more than salt and fish in the water of the Atlantic Ocean. He turned his thoughts to his job.

Siclari was one of the EP's original "Dirty Thirteen," the small group made up of a lawyer, two lieutenants, and ten detectives like himself, that was formed in 1984 to deal with New York City's growing pollution problems. Their task was to track down, investigate, and bring criminal polluters to justice. Like his fellow officers, Rocco had formerly worked on the street as a Sanitation Department collector. "It ain't all garbage," he liked to say. He knew, just as did the collector whose inner red flag went up when he saw the green garbage bags on Kingsbridge Road, that people in the city throw out more than banana peels and coffee grounds with their trash.

When the call from the Bronx came that afternoon, Rocco and his immediate boss, Lieutenant Anthony Rossano, responded.

A captain from the city Fire Department's hazardous waste division was already on the scene when the men arrived. Also alerted by the Sanita-

84

tion Department, the captain had run a field test on the material in the green bags. It was what everyone suspected, and what the building owner knew—asbestos.

Asbestos is an unusual mineral. Its tiny fibers can be molded or woven into fabric. But its primary characteristic is its nonflammability. Because asbestos won't burn and is also a poor conductor of heat, it has been used for over 2,000 years to make such things as candle wicks and cremation cloth. Modern uses include fireproof clothing for fire fighters, but its greatest application has been as insulation material. From home attics and schoolhouse ceilings to deep inside office buildings and battleships, asbestos products have been used to insulate and fireproof.

The pipes in the boiler room at 235 Kingsbridge Road had been thickly insulated with asbestos lagging. Now it lay in garbage bags on the sidewalk, encircled by a plastic banner to warn people away. The bright-orange banner read: HAZARDOUS MATERIAL. DO NOT ENTER. What no one knew about asbestos for 2,000 years was that it causes cancer. Because the asbestos had been improperly removed and then placed on the street for disposal with ordinary garbage instead of being dealt with by trained hazardous waste disposers, a crime had been committed. It was not a major crime, and certainly not one that would raise eyebrows in New York City.

Rocco ducked his head as he worked his way around the boiler room. The floor was littered with asbestos particles, and the stripped pipes, a total of 167 feet (51 m) of them, still contained stubborn

A member of the New York City Environmental Police Unit cleans up asbestos in double-layer bags at LaGuardia Airport in New York.

bits that did not come off. While he was there, an asbestos abatement inspector arrived. He took three samples from three different locations. They would be used in lab tests as evidence. The inspector gave two of the samples to Rocco.

Five o'clock had come and gone as the investigation dragged into the evening. On the street, building owner Jagmohan and the building's superintendent chatted with the authorities who had descended on this quiet corner. The building owner freely admitted that to facilitate repairs the asbestos had been removed the day before.

At about eight o'clock that evening, two Department of Environmental Protection (DEP) certified technicians arrived with a truck to remove the asbestos. The bags had already been thoroughly wet down to prevent blowing fibers from drifting through the air. The great danger from asbestos is that its tiny particles, when inhaled, cause lung cancer. The technicians donned space-age protective suits that covered them from head to foot. Appearing more like bomb-disposal experts, they gingerly carried the bags of asbestos to their truck. When the site was totally clear of the offending material, they drove off.

The building owner was cited for illegal disposition of hazardous substances and was given six summonses. Although they don't look much different from ordinary parking tickets, if the summonses were fully enforced, they would carry a maximum fine of $25,000 each, for a total of $150,000.

It would be unusual for the full force of the law to be applied in such a situation. Some kind of fine was likely, but even that would be up to the judge who heard the case. In an interview later, Lieutenant Pat Dugan, the senior environmental cop, said, "We work hard to put together a case that will stick in court. Some agencies just give tickets." The case against Jagmohan was a good one, but subsequent events changed it entirely.

A court date was set for Mr. Jagmohan and the EP unit put the case behind it. Then, on January 23, 1989, almost four months after the bags had been found on the street, Rocco Siclari scribbled a note to himself on a yellow legal pad. "Go to [a certain address], 69th St., Middle Village, Queens. Adjust dates on summons to change court date." The note was as straightforward as a reminder to pick up a loaf of bread from the store on the way home might be. The legal system, perhaps clogged by too many cases, merely wanted to change the time it would hear Mr. Jagmohan's case.

Rocco went to the address with the court summonses in hand. He chatted briefly with Mr. Jagmohan. Rocco Siclari is a kind man, even though his size can be intimidating. He speaks quietly, in a way that encourages trust. He explained why he was there.

Jagmohan coughed, apparently a chronic condition. He glanced around nervously, then spoke to Siclari. "I wish you would have spoken to me before you wrote the summons. My friend told me all I had to do was to pay you off and everything would be OK."

The man's words touched nerves that ran all the way back to the EP unit's Broadway offices.

Without knowing it, he had insulted every member of the small, elite force of "toxic cops." The crimes Jagmohan was originally charged with paled. The deeper message of his blatant bribery offer was that the EP could be bought. It was the very crime that had created the unit in the first place. When "Johnny Cash" accepted over half a million dollars in bribes to look the other way as private trash haulers illegally emptied trucks of toxic wastes in the dump he was supposed to protect, he tarnished the whole department. Years of honest work by the hardworking, dedicated EP force was being scoffed at, right in the face of one of its members.

Rocco knew the significance of what he had heard. His integrity and that of his fellow officers was on the line. He agreed to think about the offer, then he left.

Detective Rocco Siclari went immediately to his superiors and reported the incident. The Department of Investigations (DOI) Inspector General's office took over.

Acting on instructions from the DOI, Rocco arranged a payoff date with Mr. Jagmohan. On January 23, 1989, he kept it. But before he set off to meet Jagmohan, the full undercover expertise of the EP unit was brought to bear.

Rocco strapped a small radio transmitter to his body, a hidden "wire" that would broadcast his conversation with Jagmohan back to a recording unit in an unmarked van that would be parked across the street from the meeting place. Also in the van was a Panasonic WB-3250 video camera aimed through a one-way glass. Attached to it was a Panasonic A6-2400 video recorder. Whatever the two men said and did would be recorded as evidence.

## The Payoff

Once the transmitter is safely hidden on Rocco's hulking frame, and before he confronts Jagmohan, Special Investigator Mark Aronoff of the DOI asks him if he is wearing the wire of his own free will. Rocco responds with a firm yes. His pockets are emptied of money to avoid any accusations of carrying "planted" bribery money. Rocco speaks once more to establish his identity on the tape being made. "My name is Detective Rocco Siclari, Environmental Police Detective, New York Department of Sanitation." He is ready.

At three thirty-eight in the afternoon of January 23, the radio is on and the recorder running. "How do you read?" Rocco asks over the sound of background noises as he approaches his meeting place. "Five by five," is the response.

Rocco knocks on the door. A muffled voice from inside says, "Get in." The tape runs on. Rocco's voice is first.

"How do you do?" he asks.

"Sick and tired," Jagmohan answers.

The two men engage in small talk. Jagmohan makes a move.

"Don't pull out anything here," Rocco warns. "You have the summonses?"

"Yeah."

Rocco looks Jagmohan straight in the face. "What do you have in mind?"

Jagmohan shrugs. "I'm a poor man. I am willing to give you something."

Rocco nods. "Well, I gave you two hundred and fifty thousand dollars in summonses. You gotta tell me what you had in mind."

The would-be briber is uncertain. "I don't know. How much could you, ah . . ."

For the bribery attempt to stick, Jagmohan has to make an actual offer. If Rocco suggests a figure, he can be accused of soliciting a bribe. Rocco knows that. "You gotta tell me," he says.

Jagmohan is nervous. "I don't know. You know, it's the first time, so could you tell me how much you could . . ."

The confrontation is stalemated. Rocco must get Jagmohan to make an actual cash offer to destroy the summonses, but the man seems to think perhaps Rocco will set the figure. After all, why offer a large bribe when a small one might do the trick?

Rocco becomes impatient. "Well, let's go with the summons, then. You're wasting my time. I gotta go."

"Well, you tell me how much you want," Jagmohan says.

Rocco shakes his head. "I'll take the summonses back." He's getting nowhere so he speaks directly to Jagmohan. "I'm here. What do you want to do?"

The trading is over. Jagmohan knows he has to make his move. "It's tough for me to do," he says. "I got sick for this deal, man. We could get two grand. Would it be good?"

The offer has been made, but unless Jagmohan actually gives Rocco the money, there is no bribery, only an attempt. That is not good enough. But

Jagmohan does not have the money with him. He offers to write Rocco a check. The officer refuses. Only cash will do.

Another meeting is set. Rocco leaves, discouraged that the matter hasn't ended, but determined that it soon will. The following Friday the men meet again. Jagmohan's cough is worse and Rocco suggests he have it looked at. The men have established a relationship and they engage in small talk. Rocco's soft manner is reassuring. Jagmohan writes a personal check for $2,000. As they drive to a bank branch to have it cashed, they continue to chat as every word is duly taped on the recorder in the hidden van. "Look out for that guy," Jagmohan says, pointing out an unwary pedestrian to Rocco at the wheel.

The final taped segment to be filed as evidence against Jailal Jagmohan is labeled "Payoff." Jagmohan was arrested on March 15 and charged with the bribery of Environmental Police Officer Rocco Siclari. On October 2, 1989, in the United States District Court, Eastern District, Jailal Jagmohan pleaded guilty to charges of bribery of a government agent.

Department of Investigations commissioner Kevin Frawley said this about Detective Siclari and the EP unit: "The prompt reporting by this sanitation officer and his willingness to involve himself actively in the investigation deserve high praise. This is precisely the type of response we need from honest city workers to succeed in our fight against corruption in the city government."

Sanitation Department commissioner Brendan Saxton added this to the report handed to the press, lauding the action. "The illegal dumping of asbestos is a very serious crime and our Environmental Police unit spends much of its time investigating illegal disposals. In this particular case I am pleased that the officer who responded to the dumping and was subsequently offered money to look the other way refused to do so and did the right thing."

## Kids' Games

"Hey, you guys, look at this! A baby bird!"

A young boy stared with delight at the feathery ball cowering beneath a shady tree. It was a tiny bird no larger than a rolled-up sock. The tree had been its home but now it was at the mercy of whatever found it first.

The boy's young companions joined him. School in Indianapolis, Indiana, was out for the year. Vacation was in full swing. The morning was bright, but the long day ahead was still without a plan.

"A cat'll get it if we leave it," one youth said.

"It looks dead already," a second answered.

"Uh-uh," the boy who found it said. "It's alive." He picked up the small creature and held it in the palm of his hand as if it were water that would spill out if he moved.

The others studied the palmful of quivering feathers. The bird's beak opened and closed, but the boys had nothing to give it.

"Let's make a nest for it," one of the kids suggested.

Immediately the group dispersed, each of them looking for something that would protect the baby bird from harm.

One ran to the alleyway behind a local medical clinic. A fat green dumpster used to hold trash crowded against the building. The heavy metal lid had been left open. The boy chinned himself on the dumpster's side and peered in. "Oh, jeez," he muttered. He slid to the ground. "Hey, come 'ere. Look what *I* found."

The group gathered at his side, anxious to see the latest discovery.

"Boost me," the first boy said.

His buddies shoved him over the side of the dumpster. He bent down inside. When he reappeared, he held two neatly closed boxes. "They're full," he said as he handed them out. He scrambled to the ground.

The boxes were opened. In one was a number of plastic syringes, the kind doctors use to draw blood. In the other was the blood, neatly sealed in small glass vials. The baby bird was forgotten. The kids took the boxes and, not knowing exactly what they wanted to do with them, hid them in some bushes.

It wasn't long before the "treasure" was rediscovered, this time by another bunch of kids from the neighborhood. Now it was their turn. More daring than the others, the youngsters played with the needle-tipped syringes, scratching pictures in the sand as if they were pencils. The vials of liquid made perfect "grenades" which burst open when thrown against the brick wall of a building.

Thirteen kids in all toyed with the carelessly discarded waste from the medical clinic. None of them knew that some of the vials contained blood taken from AIDS patients and that the needles were used

94

to draw the blood. One boy tasted the blood. Another stepped in it. A boy and his young sister, both with open poison ivy blisters, played with it. The deadly AIDS virus may have touched seven of the thirteen.

A similar episode took place one afternoon 1,000 miles (1,600 km) away in Boardman, Ohio. There, another unlocked dumpster yielded a cache of used syringes that had been improperly discarded along with less dangerous trash. The kids stuck each other's arms, pretending they were doctors.

Again, in New York City's Harlem. This time the trash wasn't even in a dumpster but was in the street in an ordinary plastic bag. Inventively, the kids who found the needle-tipped syringes used them to play darts.

The material these innocent groups of kids found was infectious "red-bag" waste. It is the ugly mix of trash that is generated by America's 7,000 hospitals and countless laboratories, clinics, nursing homes, doctors' and dentists' offices, and other health-care facilities. Possibly a million and a half pounds (680,000 kg) of the stuff accumulates every day. As kids in three cities spread halfway across the country discovered too late, some of it ends up on the street. The question is how?

## Fly Tip

The street leading to the old Madison Avenue Bridge was quiet early that morning. The squat, inelegant span connecting the northern tip of Manhattan with the Bronx was not the kind of

Detective Adrian Willis of the New York City
Environmental Police Unit examines hospital
waste generated from Beth Israel Hospital
for potential infectious material. Detective
Willis found needles and syringes contaminated
with the AIDS virus, disposed of illegally
by the hospital. As a result of these findings,
the hospital was fined $10,000.

bridge tourists came to see. It carried serious working traffic over the Harlem River, back and forth, day after day, and it looked it. Worn, chipped, and peeling, with potholes at both ends and a steel grid deck that whined when tires raced over it, the bridge set the tone for the surrounding area. Across town, the towers of the famed George Washington Bridge sparkled with sunrise. The Madison Avenue Bridge and the streets leading to it couldn't sparkle at high noon.

A noise at the end of his block caused José Sanchez to look out the street-level door of the apartment house where he lived. Similar buildings lined the street. A hump-backed garbage truck, painted gray like a battleship instead of white like those operated by the New York City Department of Sanitation, sped around the far corner and proceeded rapidly up the street. It was headed toward the bridge.

John Alston, another apartment dweller in this residential area of low-lying brick buildings, also saw the truck. So did a Mr. Tibbs.

The three men watched as the unsavory vehicle thundered down the street. None of the men noticed one another. Their attention was fixed on the speeding truck. Like paratroopers leaping from a low-flying troop transport without wings, a succession of fat black plastic garbage bags spewed from the back of the truck and rolled along the street. The force of their impact split the thin plastic and the bags' contents scattered over the pavement like water from bursting pranksters' balloons. But it was not water.

It was already a hot day in lower Manhattan. Midsummer sun had baked the tall buildings near City Hall so that even at night they were warm. On the morning of August 17, air-conditioning was the only relief for tens of thousands of men and women who worked in area offices. It was not the kind of day the men of the Environmental Police unit at 253 Broadway appreciated. Poking noses into bags, boxes, and dumpsters of trash was never a treat, but when temperatures turned garbage into things that moved, it was awful. "We lost our noses a long time ago," Officer Joe Ward once said. It's no wonder.

Sergeant Thomas McMahon of the EP unit answered the phone in his eighth-floor cubicle. This was the summer no one in the elite investigations unit would forget. It was the summer when New York's beaches and those for 100 miles (160 km) of Atlantic shoreline were fouled with needles, syringes, and vials of blood. The call was probably one more of the hundred-per-day average the men had fielded since the reports of seaborne infectious waste first started coming in.

The voice at the other end of the phone was a long way from the beach. "I live by the Madison Street Bridge," she said. "A sanitation truck just went down our street and dumped garbage all over. There's blood in it."

McMahon doubled his attention. Everything possible was already being done to manage the waste washing up on the beaches. One more call about that would be handled appropriately, but it would not set off alarms. This call did.

More calls from the area came in. Whatever was lying on the street at the opposite end of Manhattan was serious enough to cause the people living there to do something about it. Most trash lying on New York's streets is virtually invisible unless it sticks to your shoe.

Officer Simon Manning of the EP unit, badge number 2002, was dispatched to the scene. Like the other officers of his department, he wore a gun on his belt. But what he would shoot with that morning was the camera he carried.

The street leading to the bridge was littered for at least a block. Much of the trash that had erupted from the burst bags had migrated to the gutter, blown there by the wind of passing traffic. Manning had little doubt about what kind of waste he was dealing with. Among the gutted black and gray plastic bags were lengths of plastic tubing containing a red liquid which appeared to be blood. Nearby were hypodermic needles, used swabs, plastic syringes, and a number of used scalpels, or "sharps," as needles and knives are called. "Infectious waste," Manning muttered to himself as he photographed the gutter for evidence. Public Health Law 1389-aa(1) clearly defined what constituted infectious waste, and Manning knew the law by heart. He also knew the section of the same law that tells how such waste is to be disposed of. "Either by incineration in an approved infectious waste incineration facility, by sterilization by heating in a steam sterilizer or by other decontamination technique. . . ." Dumping it on the street was not an approved means of disposal.

Manning wandered up the length of the street, his head bent low, looking for clues as he studied the scattered debris. A dog-eared issue of *Modern Health Care,* a magazine of interest to health professionals, looked as if it might yield an answer to the trash's origin. Manning read the subscription label still stuck to its front cover. "St. Luke's Hospital," it said. It was a clue, but hardly good enough for the tight kind of investigations that EP insisted on. Their job was to catch polluters and make their charges against them stick. A hospital address was much too general. Manning needed something more incriminating than that. Then he spied a small scrap of blue-stained paper. A name and a New York City address were clearly typed on it.

Some time before, Dr. Michael Albom, a dermatologist, had moved his practice from the New York University Medical Center to an office on Manhattan's posh Upper East Side at 35 East 70th Street. His staff included an office manager and a nurse.

Every business in a city has to contend with some kind of trash. The stuff that collects in wastebaskets under secretaries' desks, the rotten fruit taken from a greengrocer's stand, the scraps of cloth from a clothing manufacturer's cutting room, and the blood-stained material from a doctor's office all share a similar fate: disposal. But there is one major difference. Infectious waste from health facilities is supposed to be bagged separately from discarded appointment slips and sandwich wrappers, in pink plastic "red bags." They and the ordinary black plastic bags of trash may go out the door together, but their contents cannot be mixed. It is against the

100

law in New York City, and in a growing number of other places around the country.

The law creates a problem. Only licensed infectious-waste haulers can legally cart "red-bag" trash. Trash services without such a permit cannot carry it. Also, because such trash requires special handling and disposal, it costs more to hire a red-bag specialist.

The temptation to avoid the trouble and cost is plain to see. If an unscrupulous hauler is willing to accept red-bag waste in violation of the law, it's not unlikely that the same hauler will dispose of it any way he can. Some simply rebag the pink infectious-waste bags inside ordinary black garbage bags and take it to landfills. Another way of getting rid of trash of any kind, red-bag or plain old garbage, is to drive to an isolated location. While the truck is still in motion, usually fast motion, the back is opened and the trash flies out. This is called "fly-tipping."

Just how the trash happened to fly out of the gray unmarked sanitation truck that roared up Madison Bridge Street that August morning is not known. But there is no doubt that it did dump its ugly load in front of the curious stares of at least three witnesses. Detective Manning knew that as he placed the slip of paper with the address into an envelope for safekeeping. He also had a good idea where the trash had come from.

The thorough, step-by-step investigation that followed was completed within three weeks. An announcement from the office of the District Attorney on September 8 sums it up.

"Dr. Michael J. Albom, whose office is at 33

East 70th Street, was arrested this morning by New York City Sanitation Department police officers. He is awaiting arraignment in New York City Criminal Court on violating sections of the Public Health Law and the Environmental Conservation Law. He faces up to a year in jail and a fine of up to $5,000 on conviction."

The waste found on Madison Bridge Street had beyond a doubt come from the doctor's office. Thanks to the careful investigation by the EP, the case was successfully closed. The illegal dumping of infectious waste on an ordinary American street was just one more instance in which the ignorance and greed of a few people put the well-being and safety of everyone else in jeopardy. The actions of the officers of the EP and others like them are proof that not everyone is willing to accept that kind of behavior.

## The "E-men"

Denver, Colorado, is the headquarters of the Environmental Protection Agency Office of Enforcement, the U.S. government's own "Toxic Cops." The unit manages a special force of dedicated investigators whose job is to bring polluters to justice. And they do. In six years they have produced 385 indictments and 279 convictions. A hundred more cases are awaiting trial, and investigations are continuing around the clock.

Formed as an experiment in the early 1980s, the unit started with only twenty-three investigators. Now there are forty-eight. Spread thinly over the EPA's ten national regions, the "E-men"—so-called because FBI agents were once called "G-men"—are still too few to handle the flood of polluters who soil the planet. They are able to increase their effectiveness by training state law enforcement and environmental officials in the techniques they use to catch offenders. But in a country that generates almost 300 million tons of hazardous waste every year, there is still more than enough work to go around. Increasing the size of the unit will help, but the final answer has got to be an end to willful pollution.

Polluting the environment has been a crime since 1899, when Congress passed the Rivers and Harbors Act. Unfortunately, the law was rarely applied. As serious pollution increased, it became apparent that tougher action was required. Too often polluters were merely fined, only to pollute again. The law and its application needed teeth.

As the cost of removing and disposing wastes of every kind rose, companies with little regard for the environment often found illegal ways of getting rid of their garbage. Pouring chemical wastes into rivers has been going on since the nation was founded, one of the reasons that plants, factories, and mills were located on rivers in the first place. Pouring hazardous materials into the ground was not much different.

Since the fines that companies might have to pay if they were caught were manageable, the money could be considered as simply a part of the cost of doing business. And, as business costs can be tacked on to the price of goods, it would be

*Environmental Protection Agency agents cover contaminated soil, exposed by a bulldozer, with plastic sheeting to minimize airborne contaminates.*

the consumer—the same citizen-consumer whose country was being polluted—who would end up paying.

The Environmental Protection Agency Office of Enforcement's "bible," a booklet that grows thicker year by year as polluters are caught and tried, is testimony to the kinds of willful contaminating industry and individuals perpetrate almost daily. From leather tanners to shipping companies, lumber mills to cookie bakers, steel producers to waste management companies, the list grows longer every year. Brief clips of the lengthy charges against polluters are mute evidence of the extent of pollution deliberately dumped into the environment. Here are a few samples. Remember that they only hint at the full extent of the crime.

On four occasions discharged oil into Ohio River.

Wastewater containing sulfuric acid discharged into Woodbridge Creek.

Workers pumped dichlorobenzene, dichlormethane, toluene, and ethylbenzene into open trench.

Discharged pollutants including soaps, detergents, acids, waxes, caustic alkali, dyes and solvents from manufacturing operations into hidden pipe connected to storm sewer leading to Duwamish River.

Raw sewage dumped into Colorado River.

Endangered employees by directing them to test chemicals such as cyanide, toluene, and xylene by sniffing samples or lighting them in soft drink cans rather than by performing required chemical analysis.

There are many, many more. Each reference refers to a full story. For example, this one: "Dumping 1,000 gallons of waste containing 1,1,1-trichlorethane onto ground."

## Drum Count

Rain clouds hung heavily over the western Florida sky as Ed Fountain drove to work in Goldenrod, a suburb of Orlando. "I hope it rains someplace else," he thought. "Even Disney World would be better than here. At least all that soaks into the ground over there is water." He sighed. "Those Disney people sure know how to keep a place tidy." Disney World is one of the cleanest places on earth. Its shiny buildings and manicured streets are on the opposite side of Orlando. It was a world of difference from the kind of place Ed was driving to that August morning.

Ed turned the corner onto Forsyth Road. The plant he managed, City Industries, lay just ahead. He was uncomfortable when he went to work on days that threatened rain. He had good reason to be.

Fountain parked in the area reserved for employees of the waste-disposal company. The yard behind him was filled with an assortment of drums, tanks, and company trucks. Without having to bother counting the stored drums stacked like cans on a supermarket shelf, Ed knew there were far more than the 1,300 authorized by local law. He shook his head. The sky was growing darker. If it rained at Disney World it was not important. But Ed knew it was going to rain in Goldenrod by midday. That was important.

The waste-recycling and -transportation business on Forsyth Road had been in operation for a number of years. During that time, countless drums and truckloads of factory wastes from regional manufacturing plants had been disposed of through City Industries. The chemicals had tongue-twisting names like 1,1,1-trichlorethane, tetrachlorethylene, toluene, and xylene. Some had chillingly familiar names like arsenic pentoxide, sodium cyanide, and lead acetate. It was a witch's brew of deadly stuff, and all of it was classified as hazardous.

The owner of City Industries was Arthur Greer of nearby Maitland. He was inside when Ed Fountain entered the building where his own office was located. Greer was speaking with an employee, and his words drifted down the hall. "A rainy day is a good day to keep the drum count down," Greer was saying.

Ed shuddered. One of his primary responsibilities as plant manager was to "keep the drum count down."

The drum count was an ongoing conflict at City Industries. Authorized to store only 1,300 drums on-site, the company took on far more than that. In order to keep the place from overflowing with drums of toxic chemicals, the waste had to be disposed of. Since City Industries was in the waste disposal business, that would not seem to be a problem. However, Arthur Greer had his own ideas about how to dispose of hazardous waste. One of them was simply to dump it on the ground.

Ed Fountain knew what was coming. He had had conflicts with his boss before about what to do when they had more drums than the law allowed. On one occasion he was distressed when an unusually noxious load of waste was emptied onto the ground. Greer didn't seem to care where it went, which was straight into the soil and nearby drains. Eventually, of course, some would percolate down to the underground water table. If it ended up in someone's drinking water, well, what harm could it do?

The plant manager had spoken up to Greer about the dumping that time. Greer had looked sharply into Ed Fountain's face. "I never had any problem out of my other plant managers," he had said. "Do I see a problem out of you?" Ed didn't push the issue any further. It would have been pointless.

Greer saw Ed enter his office. He stopped talking with his employee and joined Fountain. "Ed Blasko just came back with a 1,000-gallon [about 3,800 liters] truckload of waste he picked up this morning," he said to Fountain. Ed Fountain pulled his chair away from his desk and sat down. He knew Blasko had gone to pick up the material. After all, he was the plant manager. He didn't say anything, but waited for Greer to speak.

"We're gonna need that truck, you know," Greer said to him.

Ed nodded. What he hoped would not happen was about to happen. "What am I supposed to do with the stuff that's already on the truck?" he asked. He knew there was no place to store the newly arrived toxic waste at the site. The "drum count" was already too high.

"We talked about this more than once before, Ed," Greer said, speaking very distinctly so that Fountain would have no doubt as to what he intended. "Now, do I see a problem out of you again?"

Ed's shoulders dropped. "No, not that I know of." But of course he did. Whenever the question of what to do with excess wastes came up, Ed was expected to do what the company had done long before he was employed there. He'd even let himself slip into the habit so that it became second nature. Still, he felt he had to say something. "But I'll say again, there's no place to put the stuff. It's impossible to put it anywhere on-site. I don't have any tanks for it. There's no room in the vertical storage tanks. I don't have any drums to pump it into. . . ."

Greer leaned over Ed's desk. "Blasko is gonna need that truck to pick up another load. That's the job I hired him to do." He stared straight into Fountain's eyes. "And the job I hired you to do is to take care of the stuff he brings back."

"What am I supposed to do with the stuff that's already on the truck?" Ed asked.

Greer turned toward the door. "You handle it." He walked out.

It was raining by the time Ed reached the corner of the yard where Ed Blasko's truck was parked.

"A rainy day is a good day to keep the drum count down," he muttered, repeating what he'd heard Greer say a short time earlier. Acting against his own better judgment, he pumped the big tanker dry. One thousand gallons of hazardous waste containing 1,1,1-trichlorethane flowed into the earth and nearby drains, where it mixed with other toxic wastes that had been dumped there illegally many times before. The ground under his feet was incredibly contaminated already, and Ed Fountain had just dumped a thousand gallons more.

On the other side of Orlando, the shower had passed. Thousands of tourists enjoying the marvels of Disney World stepped into the brilliant Florida sunshine. The streets and buildings glistened from their recent rinse. "How can they keep this place so clean?" a man asked his wife. Their young son knew the answer right away. "Everybody knows it's not right to litter," he said. "Especially when Mickey Mouse is watching," he added with a smile.

People like Arthur Greer and countless others like him who deliberately foul the environment and pollute the earth for personal gain are also being watched. But their watchers—government E-men, the country's "Toxic Cops"—are not as friendly as Mickey. Arthur Greer discovered that when they arrested him for knowingly disposing of toxic wastes in an illegal manner, along with thirty-two other counts of criminal activity.

Tried and convicted, Greer was sentenced to five years in prison, four years and nine months of probation, 1,000 hours of community service and a $23,000 fine. On appeal his sentence was reduced to one year and one month in prison.

The people of Florida and the United States paid, through their taxes, for the cleanup and disposal of almost 200,000 gallons (757,000 liters) of hazardous materials stored at the City Industries site. The soil and groundwater at the Forsyth Road facility was so severely contaminated that it had to be treated as hazardous waste itself. It is so polluted that it will probably stay dangerously contaminated for many years to come.

## Your Backyard

This story began in outer space, at the edge of a world few people will ever get to see. It ends in your backyard, the earth itself, a place you and everyone living on it have the privilege to see every day.

Your backyard is a giant country that is part of a world of overwhelming beauty and variety. It is a world of water and earth, of plants and creatures, of life and death, all mixed in a harmonious balance so that every part has its time and place, and every living thing has its opportunity to be fulfilled.

Mountains erode into deserts over time. Forests turn to prairies. Rivers run until they're dry. Lakes fill from melting glaciers that take 10,000 years of endless winter snows to build. Ocean shores rise up to become mountains, and the cycle goes on without end.

The genie of self-destruction—willful pollution of the planet—has been let out of the bottle. The story of earth should not be left to those who would end it. It should be in the hands of those who want to see it preserved. Until everyone joins together to prevent pollution, the job of enforcing the laws that protect the environment—an overwhelming one—is entrusted to just a few. They are the "Toxic Cops."

# BIBLIOGRAPHY

## Books

Bender, David L., and Leone, Bruno. *The Ecology Controversy.* St. Paul, Minn.: Greenhaven Press, 1981.

Block, Alan A., and Scarpitti, Frank R. *Poisoning for Profit.* New York: Morrow, 1985.

Brown, Michael H. *Laying Waste: The Poisoning of America by Toxic Chemicals.* New York: Pantheon Books, 1980.

Brown, Michael H. *The Toxic Cloud.* New York: Harper & Row, 1987.

Caplan, Ruth, and Staff of Environmental Action. *Our Earth, Ourselves.* New York: Bantam Books, 1990.

Carson, Rachel. *Silent Spring.* Greenwich, Conn.: Crest, 1962.

Coffel, Steve. *But Not a Drop to Drink.* New York: Macmillan, 1989.

Commoner, Barry. *The Closing Circle.* New York: Knopf, 1971.

Commoner, Barry. *Making Peace with the Planet.* New York: Pantheon Books, 1990.

Ehrlich, Anne H., and Paul R. Ehrlich. *Earth.* New York: Franklin Watts, 1987.

113

Epstein, Samuel S., Lester O. Brown, and Carl Pope. *Hazardous Waste in America*. San Francisco: Sierra Club Books, 1982.

Fisher, David E. *Fire and Ice*. New York: Harper & Row, 1990.

Howard, Ross, and Michael Perley. *Acid Rain*. New York: McGraw-Hill, 1982.

Keogh, Carol. *Water Fit to Drink*. Emmaus, Pa.: Rodale Press, 1980.

Kiefer, Irene. *Poisoned Land*. New York: Atheneum, 1981.

Linton, Ron M. *Terracide*. Boston: Little, Brown, 1970.

Mackarness, Richard. *Living Safely in a Polluted World*. New York: Stein and Day, 1980.

Nader, Ralph, ed., Ronald Brownstein, and John Richard. *Who's Poisoning America?* San Francisco: Sierra Club Books, no date.

Ostmann, Robert. *Acid Rain*. Minneapolis: Dillon Press, 1982.

Pawlick, Thomas. *A Killing Rain*. San Francisco: Sierra Club Books, 1984.

Regens, James L., and Robert W. Rycroft. *The Acid Rain Controversy*. Pittsburgh, Pa.: University of Pittsburgh Press, 1988.

Regenstein, Lewis. *America the Poisoned*. Washington, D.C.: Acropolis Books, Ltd., 1982.

Roan, Sharon L. *Ozone Crisis*. New York: John Wiley & Sons, 1989.

Ross, Howard, and Michael Perley. *Acid Rain*. New York: McGraw-Hill, 1982.

Schneider, Stephen H. *Global Warming*. San Francisco: Sierra Club Books, 1989.

Simon, Julian. *The Ultimate Resource*. Princeton, N.J.: Princeton University Press, 1981.

Stwertka, Eve, and Albert Stwertka. *Industrial Pollution*. New York: Franklin Watts, 1981.

Weiss, Malcolm E. *Toxic Waste—Clean-Up or Cover-Up?*. New York: Franklin Watts, 1984.

Woods, Geraldine. *Pollution*. New York: Franklin Watts, 1985.

Zipko, Stephen J. *Toxic Threat*. New York: Julian Messner, 1988.

Zwick, David, and Marcey Benstock. *Water Wasteland*. New York: Grossman Publishers, 1971.

## Magazines

### Audubon
"Doomed Canaries of Tadoussac." March 1989.
"Acid Murder No Longer a Mystery." November 1988.
"Audubon Monitors Bring Problem Home." July 1988.

### BioScience
"Acid Rain Threatens Marine Life." September 1989.
"Nitrogen Saturation in Northern Forest Ecosystems." June 1989.
"Tolerance and Stress in a Polluted Environment." February 1989.
"Ocean Dumping Revisited." December 1988.
"Who's Polluting Antarctica?" October 1988.
"Action on Anti-fouling Paints." February 1988.

### Business Week
"You Just Might Clean Up with Pollution Stocks." June 12, 1989.
"The Toxic Morass in Denver's Backyard." January 9, 1989.
"Industry Is Going on a Waste-Watcher's Diet." August 22, 1988.
"The Earth's Alarm Bells Are Ringing." July 11, 1988.

### Discover
"Toxic Avengers." August 1989.
"Wastequakes." April 1989.
"Beachless Summer." January 1989.
"Trapping Toxics in Trenches." November 1988.
"That Sucker's Gonna Cost You." May 1988.
"Fountains of Lead." May 1988.

### Forbes
"Real Life Horror Story." December 12, 1989.
"Untouchable." July 24, 1989.
"Deals That Smell Bad." May 15, 1989.

### High Technology Business
"Super Microbes Attack Hazardous Waste." July–August 1989.

"Finding a Place for Hazardous Waste." October 1988.
"The Crisis in Infectious Waste." October 1988.

## International Wildlife
"Will the Sun Ever Shine on Budapest?" September–October 1989.

## Maclean's
"A Campaign Setback." September 4, 1989.
"Dangerous Cargo." August 28, 1989.
"Keeping Toxic Track." August 28, 1989.
"Unwanted Garbage, British Port Blocks Ship with Canadian PCBs." August 21, 1989.
"Fighting Acid Rain." June 26, 1989.
"Toxins by Truckload." May 22, 1989.
"A Failed Initiative." March 20, 1989.
"Profiting from Waste." January 23, 1989.
"Our Threatened Planet." September 5, 1988.
"Warnings from the Sea." September 5, 1988.
"Poison in Poor Lands." August 1, 1988.
"Trans-border Pollution." July 3, 1989.

## National Wildlife
"Are Great Lakes Fish Safe to Eat?" August–September 1989.
"Water." February–March 1989.
"What a Mess." October–November 1988.
"Not in My Backyard." April–May 1988.

## Newsweek
"The Next Love Canal?" August 7, 1989.
"Today's Toxics: Disposal." July 24, 1989.
"Water Pollution, Visible Results." July 24, 1989.
"Yesterday's Toxics: Superfund." July 24, 1989.
"The Global Poison Trade." November 7, 1988.
"The Big Haul in Toxic Waste." October 3, 1988.
"Don't Go Near the Water." August 1, 1988.
"In Health, There Are No Borders." August 1, 1988.
"Toxins, Toxins Everywhere." August 1, 1988.
"Cleaning Up." July 24, 1988.

"Blood in the Water." July 18, 1988.
"Stretched to the Limit." July 11, 1988.

## Oceans
"Coastal Waters in Jeopardy." March–April 1989.
"The Dredge Spoil Disposal Dilemma." November–December 1988.
"TBT on its Way Out." September–October 1988.
"Copper Ore Pollutes Marine Life Near Wreck." July–August 1988.
"Last Summer at the Jersey Shore." July–August 1988.
"Sanctuaries or Garbage Dumps?" July–August 1988.
"Stop Sewage Sludge Dumping." May–June 1988.
"EPA December Decision Ends Sea Burns." March–April 1988.

## Omni
"Bungle in the Jungle." September 1989.
"Troubled Water." September 1989.
"Seagate." June 1989.
"Sea of Trouble." April 1989.
"The Trashing of America." February 1988.
"Watergate." February 1988.

## Reader's Digest
"Kids Crusade to Save Our Streams." June 1989.
"Cry of the American Coast." December 1988.
"Swamped by Our Own Sewage." January 1988.

## Science News
"Where Acids Reign, Do Dying Stands of Bavarian Timber Portend the Future of Polluted U.S. Forests?" July 22, 1989.
"Warning, If You Eat Great Lakes Fish." May 13, 1989.
"New Accord Would Control Waste Exports." April 1, 1989.
"Cistern Water, Soft and Corrosive." March 25, 1989.
"Unexpected Leakage through Landfill Liners." March 18, 1989.
"U.S. Ratifies International Nitrogen Oxide Treaty." November 19, 1988.

"Antarctic Research Requires Costly Cleanup." October 22, 1988.
"Waste Wells Implicated in Ohio Quake." August 27, 1988.
"First World Estimate of Metal Pollution." May 4, 1988.
"Forest Declines, Is Mighty Moss to Blame?" April 30, 1988.
"New Acid Rain Threat Identified." April 30, 1988.
"Trashes to Ashes, All Fall Down." February 6, 1988.
"Water Contents Hard to Swallow?" January 16, 1988.

## Scientific American
"Letters." January 1989.
"The Challenge of Acid Rain." August 1988.

## Sea Frontiers
"Antarctic Pollution." May–June 1989.
"Crow's Nest." November–December 1988.

## Sierra
"A Chemical War on Water." May–June 1989.
"The Children's Cleanup Crusade." March–April 1989.
"Wretched Refuse Off Our Shores." January–February 1989.
"Hugh Kaufman, EPA Whistle Blower." November–December 1988.
"Runoff Runs Amok." November–December 1988.
"Broken Promises." May–June 1988.
"Unwelcome Visitors Sully Crater Lake." January–February 1988.

## Smithsonian
"Phenomena, Comment and Notes." September 1988.
"Plastic Reaps a Grim Harvest in the Oceans of the World." March 1988.

## Time
"A Big Stink in the Pigeon." June 6, 1988.
"Something Fishy about Acid Rain." May 9, 1988.
"Into the Pipeline." March 27, 1988.
"The Greening of the USSR." January 2, 1988.
"The Dirty Seas." August 1, 1988.
"Season of Death." June 13, 1988.

## U.S. News and World Report

"Enviro-Cops on the Prowl for Polluters." October 9, 1989.
"Stopping Coastline Pollution at the Sewer and the Farm." August 21, 1989.
"At the Beaches This Summer, the Dirty Word is Plastics." July 17, 1989.
"Our Dirty Air." June 12, 1989.
"Would You Believe $16.67 an Hour to Scrub Rocks?" April 17, 1989.
"Uncle Sam's Toxic Folly." March 27, 1989.
"Superfund, Superflop." February 6, 1989.
"The New Midnight Dumpers." January 9, 1989.
"Perestroika vs. a Growing Wasteland." December 5, 1988.
"Dirty Job, Sweet Profits." November 21, 1988.
"Good News for Cleanup Crews." November 21, 1988.
"Good Jobs Are Going to Waste." September 12, 1988.
"Why a Flood of Filth Laps the Beaches." August 22, 1988.
"What Goes Up Must Come Down." July 25, 1988.
"Yes, They Mind If We Smoke." July 25, 1988.

## World Press Review

"The Sea Has Its Limits." June 1989.
"Canada's White Whales Are Dying." January 1989.
"The North's Garbage Goes South." November 1988.
"The North Cesspit." October 1988.

## Interviews

Martin J. Wright, Deputy Assistant Director, U.S. Environmental Protection Agency, Office of Criminal Investigations, January 1990.
Attorney Daniel Millstone, N.Y.C. Department of Sanitation, Department of Investigations, January 1990.
Lieutenant Pat Dugan, N.Y.C. Department of Sanitation, Department of Investigations, January 1990.
Detective Rocco Siclari, N.Y.C. Department of Sanitation, Department of Investigations, January 1990.
Case files provided by N.Y.C. Department of Sanitation, Department of Investigations and U.S. Environmental Protection Agency, Office of Criminal Investigations.

# INDEX

124

# ABOUT THE AUTHOR

D. J. Arneson writes books for young and adult readers in a Connecticut studio surrounded by unspoiled nature—a daily reminder of the way our earth can be if we care.